LOVE
@ DALAL STREET

LOVE
@ DALAL STREET

DR. SANDIP SANE/NIHARIKA SINGH

PARTRIDGE
A Penguin Random House Company

To order additional copies of this book, contact
Partridge India
000 800 10062 62
orders.india@partridgepublishing.com

www.partridgepublishing.com/india

Dedicated to my parents, wife Shubhada and my little daughter 'Yana'

Dr. Sandip Sane

Dedicated to my husband Late Mr. Brajesh . . . . U reside in my heart . . . .

Niharika Singh

Acknowledgement

The book has two authors but multitude of collaborators.

We are profoundly grateful to all those, who in one way or the other have inspired us to come out with an idea where a complicated subject like stock market could be explained using a storyline.

Author—Niharika owes her writings to her late husband Brajesh, who always inspired her to scale new heights and always motivated her to be the best.

Author—Dr. Sandip Sane owes a lot to his wife Shubhada who helped in conceptualising the story, intertwining the technical part and bearing tantrums at times with great patience.

We profoundly thank Ms Varada Mahajani for proof reading.

We also owe a debt of gratitude to all Authors who wrote books, articles, research papers on stock market and securities. Without the use of their collective cumulative knowledge, completion of the book could not have happened.

A special thanks to Parents, Family members and Friends for giving moral support and believing in us.

We are also very thankful to the Management of IIMS Pune, our organisation for making available all required resources needed in completion of the book.

The project would have been impossible without the skilled team from Partridge Publishing who nurtured the book at every stage and turned pile of papers into a finely polished work of art.

Dr. Sandip Sane
Ms Niharika Singh

Contents

Call 1: "Hello, Thank you so much sir . . . . its all yur wishes. Yes, I will definitely come to meet you. Ok. bbyee . . ." says Mr. Ranade while checking in the New Delhi Airport.

Call 2: "Really, how was it? Oh Great . . . Thanks a lot, k . . . i will call u back . . ."

Call 3: "Yes, speaking . . . . oh thank u so much . . . ."

Call 4: "Ohhh hiiii, hwzz u? Em fine u tell . . . Really! u read it . . . . hws it? Great yaar thanks a lot, it was just impossible without ur help . . . . yuppp . . . . sure pakka . . . . let's catch up coming Sunday . . . Cool hahaha . . . yupp . . . ok then . . . bbyee, tc . . ."

Standing in front of Singapore International Airport, Mr. Ranade was busy on cell phone, enjoying the congratulations and greetings in short praises from his relatives, friends and colleagues in fact everyone . . . . while he passed through all the formalities, from airport entry, luggage check, boarding pass, long queues for departure immigration clearance on passport, followed by hateful time taking security checks. Sitting on chair, he looked at his watch which clearly indicated that he had an hour to cherish 'The Moment'. The moment was not an ordinary one but was a day, an hour he had long long dreamt of. He ordered a capuccino at the Singapore Airline cafeteria and soon he was served the same, which had a smiley on its surface that reminded him of his students, who always greeted him with the similar smile on their faces.

While sipping his coffee, Prof. Ranade started thinking that few days back nobody knew him but now everyone knows him as The Prof. Ranade, The Man Booker Prize Award Winner . . . this feeling filled him with pride and emotion and he felt his eyes moist.

Of Course! How can he forget his journey from a mango man, a common man to The Man Booker Prize Winner . . . Indeed it was a great feeling which made his heart heavier. He was one of the lucky guy to get one. He owe his life to his students, he owe his today to 'them', he owe that "moment" to 'them' . . . he drowned himself in the cyclone of similar thoughts.

Mr. Ranade suddenly got distracted by a loud, screaming, female voice . . .

"OMG!!! I simply just can't bel . . . believe it."

When he turned around, he saw a girl in a short orangish kurti, light blue coloured skirt with a multicoloured stoll. Brown straightened hair, half tied with a puff and few falling on face, her fingers struggled to set them aside. With a blue framed specs and a long hand bag on one shoulder gave her a look of a perfect journalist. To the great surprise of Prof. Ranade, she was coming towards him taking fast steps.

"Are you Mr. Ranade, The Booker Prize Award Winner?" She asked in a super excited tone.

"Yes" he said.

"Hiiiiiiii, u donno me but ema great great fan of yours . . . u know i have read your book and it's just AWESOME! I have been following u since the prize distribution ceremony . . . i tried to get your number but was unable to do so . . . ." she seemed like to have no end to her ongoing talks, "u know i like the way you had described your characters, you know i like . . . ." suddenly she stopped, observing that Professor was quite blank and then she realized she didn't introduce herself.

"Oh em so sorry, am so stupid na . . . . yeah this is inborn quality of mine . . . actually my mom also says that i have no mind, my father always keeps on asking me to shut my mouth . . . but you tell me, is it possible to do so? . . . atleast not for me . . . . this is the reason my bro always fights with me . . . because he expects me to shut my mouth, which I never do . . ."

Mr. Ranade was disinterested in the stupid talks of that girl. Since, the time for flight was approaching, Mr. Ranade looked at his watch and started preparing to leave or perhaps he didn't want himself to be tortured anymore by useless talks of that stupid girl.

Suddenly the girl said, "Oh!! wait wait! Sir where r u goin, i mean!! u can't leave me like this . . ."

"Why!!!"

"I came here just to meet you and you are going now."

"Yes, because I have to go back to Pune"

"Noope, but i havnt yet completed my talks." Suddenly her blooming face drooped down and her nose got reddened, voice a bit crumpled as if she was about to cry.

Mr. Ranade was moved by sudden change in her behavior and tried to soothe her and asked, "Ok . . . tell me, how can I help you.?"

"I want to take your interview" wiping her eyes.

"But its now time for my flight. How is it possible now?" Mr. Ranade said in a soft voice.

She thinks for a while, makes a call, and takes permission for leave for a week. Immediately rushes towards the ticket counter. Mr. Ranade was not able to understand what was up. And then there was another surprise in store for him as she comes back running with an electrifying smile and a ticket to Mumbai.

"Oh . . . shitt!" said Mr. Ranade to himself.

"Cool na!! now i will get enough time to talk to you" she smiled and said while playing with her hair.

Both of them then started to move towards the flight. They were guided to their seats by an amazingly beautiful humble airhostess to the business class. Mr. Ranade's seat was in front and two rows back was hers (The Journalist Girl). He was quite relaxed that now she won't be able to disturb him. And then he bent his head on the comfortable and cosy chair to take rest and closed his eyes. Not even a few seconds had passed, he was disturbed by the same female voice, who else 'The Journalist Girl' perhaps she managed to get the seat beside him. She smiled cutely but he felt irritated. He cursed himself why he was moved by her momentary emotional drama turning out to be a trauma. They were asked to fasten their seat belts. It was sharp 10:00 A.M. and soon the plane took off and in a few seconds they were above the clouds and so was she, on the seventh cloud, as she was sitting beside a person whom she admired most. She had read all books written by him.

After having snacks and ice tea, she again started talking to professor, rather irritating him but this time she was more polite and gentle. "Sir, I am Saloni, em a journalist at BVP news, came here for international assignments and project.

"Ahhh!!! there i was correct, my guess was almost right . . . she is journalist" thought Professor and she started.

"I read your book and since then I had extreme desire to meet you and know about you. Actually I have taken you as a part of my study for this summer project. I want to know what motivated you to write such a story which infotains the reader and depicts about the student-teacher relationship. Is it a true story or a fiction? How long did it take you to write this book? What was there in your mind while writing this book? How did you get the idea of writing on this subject? How do you feel accomplishing such great feat? Em sure em not irritating u . . . em i . . . ?" and thus she bombarded him with many questions.

Though Mr. Ranade was initially irritated by her continuous questioning, but the questions gave him the opportunity to go back into the ocean of his beautiful and most cherished memories . . . hence now he didn't mind much.

"Well, this book is . . . ." Mr. Ranade replied in a thoughtful manner seemed as if he was ready to plunge into the waves of time but he said "I will tell you the story first, then you can guess if its fiction or real, Ok". Saloni agreed.

And he started the narration . . . .

What is in it for me (WIIIFM) . . .

. . . . It was a new day with sun beaming bright as usual but with new soothness accompanied by a little drizzling that made the climate more pleasant, lush green grass carpet, campus more energized, faculties more enthusiastic, reason being the first day of 1st semester management students in International Institute for Advance Management Studies (IIAMS).

Senior students were also quite excited by seeing their juniors; perhaps they had plans of ragging them. Out of all Kapil Sisodiya (popularly known as "Kaps") and Vihaan Saxena (Popularly known as "Vav"), who were considered as the macho dude of the college, were the most desirable seniors. Most of the junior gals wanted and were approaching them for notes, guide and assistance. They were quite amused by the fan following they enjoyed or rather enjoying.

Kapil, is an intelligent guy, arrogant, 5'10" heighted, dusty texture with brown eyes, curly hair and strongly build and that is the reason for his popularity. Contrast to Kapil, Vihaan is a humble, kind, 6 ft, fair color, black hair, cute smile guy which makes him more charming and adorable. Both Kapil and Vihaan are opposite but still their friendship is popular and strong.

Kapil and Vihaan both were observing the junior students, or to correct, girl students. "Hey Kaps, look she is beautiful . . . . and that one with the specs seems her favourite place would be library." "Oh!! Look at her . . . her face looks over powdered . . . . shall i tell her not to overdo it . . ."

"Hey!! Why don't you speak anything . . . ?"

"Nothing to speak, they all are gonna be in my fans list, but . . . ." said Kapil.

"But . . . . what??"

"No one is like her . . . ."

"OMG . . . . u never told me about her, you have one? Kaps, the hunk of our college has one, who is that gorgeous lady . . ."

"Oh come on . . . its not like that . . . . I don't hv any."

"But jxt nw, u said."

"I just saw her once . . . . no twice . . . . no no thrice . . . . i mean i dunno . . ."

"What r u saying, i don't get u??"

"U won't believe it . . . I dunno it was my dream or reality . . . ." suddenly Kapil was interrupted by the bell and they both moved towards the classroom for their lectures. "to be continued . . ." Kapil said and winked.

The Insititute is famous for its Post Graduate management Program but besides the core program, the institute also provides a certification course in Security analysis and Portfolio management. This certificate programme was the most sought after program and one of the USP of the institute offered to both seniors and juniors.

The certification program was a highlight in IIAMS campus because it's been taught by one of the best faculties of institute, Dr. (Prof.) Shashank, a renowned Professor with vast knowledge on his subject. At a very young age of 35, he had established himself as a master of the subject. He is a doctorate in Finance and Post doc in Stock and Securities. Besides his teaching experience, he also worked as financial analyst in Banking sector. But above all he is a very dynamic, energetic, smart and handsome, which makes him more popular among the students. Students get charmed by his soft spoken language mixed with great knowledge accompanied by his unique body language. He has many fans following on twitter and facebook as well. And of course last but not the least, he is still single. He is recognised as one of the best faculties of the institute. He in himself is a brand.

The students proceeded towards the classroom as the bell rang for the lecture.

It was the first lecture of SAPM. Most of the students were from second year, because generally the first year students don't have enough knowledge on the topic and they aren't prepared for the same.

As Prof. Shashank entered the class room, students welcomed him with a corporate clap, which was loud enough and showed the students' admiration for him. Students were all charged up he could sense that.

Prof. Shashank, showing gratitude, said, "We are going to learn Securities and Portfolio Management in our certificate course. Are you ready for it?" There was a huge and loud yes from the students.

Prof Shashank said" Before we start, let me tell you an anecdote,
A minister dies and is waiting in line at the Pearly Gates. Ahead of him is a guy with sunglasses and dressed in a loud shirt, leather jacket, and jeans. Saint Peter

addresses this guy, "Who are you, so that I may know whether or not to admit you to the Kingdom of Heaven?"

The guy replies, "I'm Joe Cohen, stockbroker, of New York City."

Saint Peter consults his list. He smiles and says to the stockbroker, "Take this silken robe and golden staff and enter the Kingdom of Heaven."

The stockbroker goes into Heaven with his robe and staff, and it's the minister's turn. He stands erect and booms out, "I am Joseph Snow, pastor of Saint Mary's for the last forty-three years."

Saint Peter consults his list. He says to the minister, "Take this cotton robe and wooden staff and enter the Kingdom of Heaven."

"Just a minute," says the minister. "That man was a stockbroker—he gets a silken robe and golden staff but I, a minister, only get a cotton robe and wooden staff? How can this be?"

"Up here, we work by results," says Saint Peter. "While you preached, people slept; his clients, they prayed."

Students started laughing. Professor said "So Friends give right and correct advice and to do that u need to know stock market and its operations in detail.

Prof. Shashank enquired "I suppose you all are sure, why you want to do this course and particularly the subject on Stock market". There were many answers, some said, we like Stock market, some wanted certificate, however most of them were confused, they had no answers why they were doing, and perhaps some of their seniors had done this course, so they were doing.

Shashank sat on the chair and again asked "Have you heard of FM Radio "WIIFM", did anyone listen or tuned to WIIFM anytime?". Students knew about Radio Mirchi, Red FM but no one have ever heard of what the professor was talking about and they started whispering, WIIFM'.

Shashank was amused and he jumped up the chair and with his mischievous smile started again "WIIFM is nothing but acronym for **What Is In it For Me**". "I would never get myself into something until i know what benefit I will get from it. I would suggest you to follow this formula cause it will set GOAL for you and you would be knowing what you can achieve once you finish a stated task".

Shashank was a prolific speaker and fantastic motivator. He knew the first impression even though is not last impression but surely is lasting impression and he was ready to spend enough time in explaining his audience what benefit they can get if they go ahead with the Certificate course.

Shashank said "The basic simple fact is, we all are doing PG in management, Certificate courses and so many other things to ensure that we have decent career. So our 1st session also needs to be on the opportunities which stock market offers for us".

Suddenly there was a query from one of the students, Kapil, "Sir I know lot of stock broking firms but will they take rookies like us?."

"Yup . . . , Its not only Stock Broking Firms but plenty of other sectors like MF companies, Banks, Rating Agencies, they have huge requirements for freshers as well as people with experience. However, one thing is clear you need to be USTAD and expert in your subject", said Prof Shashank.

Shashank was at his best. He picked up a book, while sitting on the chair, he said to the class, the book is like a Job Market. He picked a page and tried to insert into the book. He was able to do it as the book was loosely held. He said 10 years back market was similar to book held now, you could enter in between but now the market has changed. He pressed the book and then tried to insert page between the pages of the book which he could not. He asked, "Where is the place for the page to enter?" Nobody could answer. Finally he said "it's either on top of book or at the end of it. The Job Market is tight and you have to be either at the top or bottom, it's up to you to decide where you want to be. To be at the top one has to master the subject". Students got the message and were determined to do well.

"I will give you all information on various career opportunities in financial markets and the subject. But with that you also have to promise me, you will master the art of investment in stock market and other securities". The students shouted back "YES SIR, We'll DO THAT". It was something like a colonel ordering his soldiers and getting reply with thundering voice.

Shashank, getting a bit exhausted, opened the slide share showing about the companies, job opportunities and career in the Financial Market, which was now visible on the laptops of all students through programmed instruction . . .

You can be . . . .

Fund Managers are the individuals responsible for making portfolio decision for mutual fund. The eligibility criteria for being a Fund Manager is a professional degree like MBA/PGDM in finance and needs to have interest in Stock market and Fund Management. Salary: 2 lacs-50 lacs pa and above.

Distributors An Individual or corporation serving as principle underwriter of mutual fund's shares, buying shares directly from the fund, and reselling them to other investors. Salary: 2-10 Lacs pa.

Dealers They act as intermediary between the customer and the stock market. He advises customers on purchase and sale of stocks. Salary: 1.8-3 lacs pa.

Career with Regulatory Bodies, Rating Agencies and Depositories

Regulatory and Rating agencies require professionals from varied backgrounds; finance, accounting, auditing, investment, credit rating, consultancy, mutual funds, law, derivatives products etc.

Career in Depositories

Deposit record, maintain and authenticates paperless trading of financial securities. Depository also act as clearing houses and provide services related to DMAT account. Examples of depositories working in India are; National Securities Depositories Ltd. (NSDL), Central Depositories Services Ltd. (CDSL) and Stock Holding Corporation of India (SHCIL). Degree like CA/ICWAI/CS/CFA/MBA with some experience in stock exchanges, brokerage firms, banks and financial services companies from reputed institutes/universities can make career in it.

Research and Consultancy

Investment firms has equity research department for Mutual Funds, FIIs, institutional investors. Broking houses hire research specialists. Print and electronic media also offer opportunities for professionals' expert advice on stock investment and volatility.

There are various job opportunities available who has got knowledge in stock market.

Now let's have a look at some institutions offering programmes/courses in investment management. Prof. Shashank clicked on the second slide that talks about few of the job opportunities available for the fresher's and experienced once.

As the slides ended students were really amazed and excited by the job opportunities available to them in the market. The professor ended the session with the information that in next lecture he will discuss about how to make investment decisions. Perhaps this was his strategy to prepare the students mentally for the next session.

Soon the bell rang and all the students came out of the class. And here ends the lecture, Prof Shashank, who was actually exhausted, also left the classroom. He was able to create the impression which he intended to. Nisaa, who always was one of the most obedient students noticed the tiredness of Professor Shashank and she just came to him and said, "Thank you so much sir, for the wonderful lecture, by the way u look exhausted today, sir." He smiled meekly and replied, "Yes, dear . . . extra work . . . By the way thanks for the compliment" "Ok, sir. Take care. Bbye" Said Nisaa and left. All the students including Ashok, Kapil, Vihaan, Chhabi and Nisaa went to the canteen to have something.

They moved towards the canteen, and reached at their all time favourite table, which automatically gets reserved they being seniors. Canteen was full of students bustling with all kinds of activities. Some were enacting how the Professor speaks; few were planning for movies and so on.

As they reached their place Chhabi immediately ordered Kapil's favourite 'Madrasi coffee' strong and less sugar for him and for Vihaan as well. Kapil knew that Chhabi secretly loved and cared for him, but he never paid heed to her. Kapil made a cold response whereas, Vihaan thanked Chhabi for her favour. Vihaan though many times advised Kapil to be kind towards her but he never listened to him, on the other hand Chhabi never expected anything from Kapil. Her feelings were one way. Vihaan started thinking about Chhabi. Chhabi, dark black eyes, fair, cute smile, pretty girl, height 5'1", long hair, intelligent, a good singer, kind hearted and soft spoken girl. She looked different from others in her patiala and kurti but still cute and charming. But perhaps she wasn't Kapil's type.

Thus Vihaan was dragged by his own thoughts, where Kapil was busy in interacting with the juniors who approached them, especially girls, of course to impress them. He came back and sat on the chair with Vihaan. Suddenly Vihaan's thoughts broken as he was distracted by Kapil's voice, "Hey Vav!! ur coffee is getting cold and what are you thinking?"

"About 'her'" with a wink.

Kapil got the hint about whom he is talking . . . he started narrating . . .

A Mystery Girl

"Few days ago, I had been to Bombay Stock Exchange, just to visit the place. It was a steaming hot day with the bright sun on head, everyone was sweating, me too. As I reached in front of the building there was a check post where we were supposed to show our id proof and then only we get permission to enter. I went near to the check post, handed over my pan card to the security man standing there, as he was busy in doing paper work . . . My eyes went to a girl coming out of the building . . . . A cute and small faced girl with big eyes. Her innocence was visible on her face but her walking style depicted her boldness. She was in orange spaghetti top below and cotton white translucent shirt over it, with a coffee brown cartridge jeans and a cream coloured peep toes. Her shiny brown hair were blowing on her face and shoulder, she carried a brown leather bag. In that scorching warm weather she looked like a cool breeze of air . . . . resetting her hair, she was coming towards me . . . . I kept on staring at her . . . . she passed me and a fresh smell of roses surrounded me . . . . I was just hypnotized by her smell . . . . I followed her . . . . though at the back of my ear I could hear the sound of security man calling me and shouting over me but at that moment all I wanted to do was to follow her . . . . she kept on walking and I kept on following her . . . . she went towards right, I too . . . . then she went straight I don't remember how long i followed her but suddenly i reached a crowdy place . . . . and she disappeared there. I couldn't see her anywhere . . . . she was not present anywhere . . . . I was surprised to see where she had gone . . . . Soon i found myself lost, I wasn't able to locate my position, but immediately i booked an auto and went back to BSE to take my pancard, that security man abused me for I was following a her. I also felt a bit ashamed.

I took the same auto and went to the bus stop to return to Pune. Soon I got the bus for Pune . . . I was tired and soon fell asleep while thinking about my dream girl. After a couple of hours, I was waken up by the loud voices of hawkers and I found that the bus had stopped at lonavala for a break . . . .

To my great surprise, I saw the same girl in the same dress, sitting at the first seat of the bus but before I could say or believe my eyes she got down the bus . . . and now I could see her near a shop. Perhaps she went there to purchase something to eat.

Soon the bus honked for the passengers and driver started the bus. I asked the conductor to wait for the girl passenger who sat on the first seat, and had gone outside to purchase. To my great surprise, the conductor said, there was no girl sitting on that seat.

I was really shocked to hear that and when I watched outside the bus she was'nt there. I wasn't able to understand, whether it was my dream or was my hallucination.

But whatever it was, she was the one of my type . . . . I wanted girl of that type, her beauty, her style, her confidence . . . . I thought have fallen in love with her at the first sight . . . ." Kapil was again drowned in her thoughts.

"hmmm . . . . hello Mr. Kaps . . . this was just your dream . . . . or might be your dream girl . . . . the way you are narrating, it doesn't sound like a girl but more like a horror story, look, think she might be a ghost and you only saw her . . . so . . . . just beware . . ." Vihaan tried to make fun of his experience.

"You rascal . . . . just wait . . ." Kapil also got pinched and they started kidding, beating and playing with each other.

Learning with Investment Decisions . . . .

The second day of the certificate program brought good strength of students, that shows the powerful effect of professor's first lecture. Today students were more curious for the lecture, as now they were well aware that what are the benefits they can get out of this course. Some were ready with the queries and some with the reference books and few with reports to discuss with professor. Some have searched for the probable investment decisions to be made.

And the ringing of bell was followed by Prof. Shashank's entry. Students welcomed him with a corporate clap, which was louder showing the students' enthusiasm. Professor looked energetic, charged to take the stage. He was oozing with ample of information which he wanted to share. His eyes shone in brightness.

He was just about to start but before he could say anything Kapil shouted, "Sir how to make right Investment decisions?".

Professor replied "There's nothing right or wrong. One has to make Investment decisions based on his requirement and risk taking capacity. For example the Investment planning of a young person who recently got into job and earning decent salary will be different from the one who is about to retire.

"But before getting into this we need to understand what the major assets are where we can invest. Broadly speaking the investment is done in Real Assets or Financial Assets."

"Sir, So Real Assets means something which we can touch." Chhabi said which was interrupted by a sweet voice, "Sir, May I please come in." Everyone started staring towards the door.

There was a flamboyant girl standing, in a tube top covered by shrugs, cargos and puma shoes. Brown curly hair seemed as if they were not even properly combed . . . thin and tall, piercing on nose and ears, carrying a bag and a pink colored tab with earphone in her ears, chewing gum seemed as if she was a female macho . . . .

She repeated "Sir, may I please come in?" Prof Shashank replied, "This is not the 1 st sem class, its certificate programme on SAPM. Perhaps you are at the wrong place." She said confidently, "No, sir am at right place and i have also enrolled for this certificate programme."

"Well, then you are welcome. Please come." As she came inside Kapil was shocked to see her . . . . his mouth was wide open . . . eyes stucked to her . . . . he was just frozen . . . . Vihaan who said beside Kapil said, "What happened Kaps, Did u see the ghost or what?" "Yes!! I did" said Kapil . . . .

"What??" Vihaan laughed slowly.

"Yes damn it . . . . she is the one . . . ."

"who?"

"The dream girl"

"Don't tell me . . . . r u sure . . . . Do the ghosts also take lectures???" Vihaan humoured.

"Shut upp . . . am serious. She is my dream girl . . . ."

"Best of luck then . . . . dear . . . ." Vihaan winked. But Kapil was still not ready to believe his eyes.

Everyone was astonished to see a 1st sem girl in the certificate programme. She went and sat on the first bench which was left empty. Prof Shashank asked her name, she said, "Sir, I am Sharon." "Vow!!, what a voice . . ." murmured Kapil and Vihaan smiled.

"Ok, so we were discussing about Real assets and Financial assets, Yes Chhabi you were saying something."

"Yes sir, So can we say that Real Assets mean something which we can touch, which is tangible and Financial assets are those which is not tangible and is just a promise, for example amount to be received after insurance policy once it is matured. Am i right sir?" Chhabi added and glanced and smiled at Kapil, which he ignored.

"Yes you are right but let me give you another way to understand." He opened the slide share:

Real Asset is nothing but an assets which has intrinsic value and is not somebody else's liability. eg Watch, Camera, Real Estate.

Financial Assets is an asset or paper assets which is someone else's liability. eg Stock, Bonds, Currencies.

Prof Shashank this time sat on the chair and started explaining "Financial assets generally loses its value when inflation rises however physical assets or Real assets are not much affected by Inflation. The Wall street or Dalal Street for matter of fact is always biased towards Financial Assets. The reason being that they are into business of manufacturing and trading Financial Assets."

Kapil asked "Sir you said Financial assets are affected by inflation and Real assets are not, how's that possible?" This time he was of course trying to show off. Vihaan can't resist his smile at Kapil's behaviour.

Shashank said "This is a very simple question, if anyone gives answer, he will get two Cadbury silk in my next Lecture".

Cadbury Silk really acted as catalyst and there were answers flying from one end of the class to other. Finally Sharon rose after having dined with her nails and making all analysis in mind started giving the answer." Sir . . . , Real assets are not affected by inflation because their prices rise with inflation and in case of Financial Assets the profitability of the entity reduces and so they are affected adversely".

"Bravo Bravo, you deserve a silk Cadbury, no one could answer this question ever before . . .", Shashank shouted, "you are right but let me rephrase it for the benefit of the class". Along with Prof. Shashank everyone in the classroom were pleasantly surprised to hear the 1st sem girl giving answers. "hmm . . . . beauty with the brain . . . ." Vihaan informed Kapil as if he was selecting her for him. All Kapil could do was to see his dream girl in reality.

Professor showed the slide:

Real Assets are not affected by Inflation because it has been built in mechanism to counter inflation. For example if the inflation increases automatically the price of Real Assets like watches, Real Estate, Cars, Cameras etc will also increase and so the margins will be maintained. Whereas when it comes to Financial Assets, the rise of inflation increases the costing of the product thus reducing the margins and ultimately affecting the profitability adversely. Thus as profits are reduced the stock market gives thumbs down and the market falls.

"What are the avenues or instruments available in the market for investment?" asked Kapil. Kapil was excited as he was sure that he is up for a ball and will be soon noticed by his dream girl.

Shashank said "Let us find out from the class, i am sure you know all of them, let me show you.". Shashank showed the slides again.

Sr. No Instruments for Investment	Classes
Stock Financial	Asset
Bond Financial	Asset
FD/PO Financial	Asset
Real Estate Real	Assets
Commodity Real	Assets
Currency	Financial
Gold/Silver	Real/Financial

Prof Shashank said" However the gold and silver are hybrid type i.e. in the time of inflationary environment the Gold and silver acts like a currency and in non inflationary time they tend to be commodity". Professor coughed, Sharon immediately passed him her water bottle. He took a sip, said thanks to Sharon and continued . . . .

Professor said "Now let us understand the Financial market as whole."

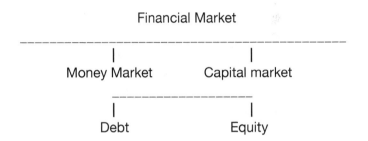

"Financial markets can mainly be classified into money markets and capital markets.

Instruments in the money markets include mainly short-term, marketable, liquid, low-risk debt securities with maturity less than a year.

Capital markets, in contrast, include longer-term and riskier securities, which include bonds and equities. There is also a wide range of derivatives instruments that are traded in the capital markets. Both bond market and money market instruments are fixed-income securities but bond market instruments are generally of longer maturity period as compared to money market instruments. Thus in capital market the maturity period is more than a year.

The equities market can be further classified into the primary and the secondary market.

Derivative market instruments are mainly futures, forwards and options on the underlying instruments, usually equities and bonds." Shashank explained as if everyone understood each and every word.

'Sir, it was a bouncer and way over our head, there was no chance of touching it, please explain us in simple language' Vihaan said meekly

Nisaa also gave similar gesture . . . biting her nails . . .

"Don't worry this was a dip test, i just wanted to give you, hang of all that is in store when we get into the depth of Stock Market" said Prof Shashank.

"Now before venturing into Money Market and the Capital market, let us understand the difference between Primary and Secondary market".

Prof. Shashank started explaining and played the slides . . . .

'A primary market is that segment of the capital market, which deals with the raising of capital from investors via issuance of new securities. New stocks/ bonds are sold by the issuer to the public in the primary market called an Initial Public Offering (IPO).
Example: Maruti Udyog Ltd.'s offer in 1999 was an IPO because it was for the first time that Maruti Udyog Ltd. offered securities to the public.

The secondary market is the financial market in which securities are traded after the initial offering. Gauged by the number of issues traded. The over the counter market is the largest secondary market.

Prof. Shashank started explaining how trading is done in Secondary market.

Nisaa was up with her notebook, fingers in her mouth excited as usual wanted to jot down anything which comes out of professors' mouth. She also had some secret . . . which no one knew about it.

Chhabi was calm but alert. She always wanted to answer first and be in the good books of Professor. Of course her other good book was Kapil which she read him silently and lovingly.

Sharon was attending the lectures quietly, chewing gum in her mouth and playing with pen, which was a bit arrogant on part of a student. Kapil was continuously observing her and tried to impress her so that she should also be the member of his fans list, declining the fact that he himself was impressed by her. But perhaps she was in her own world.

Suddenly Ashok got excited and said "Sir i can save Rs.1000 per month, can i invest in stock market". By the way, Ashok was also amongst one of the silent admirer of Sharon.

Sharon replied "Yes, why not. I will tell you what is to be done". She started saying. Ashok made a sigh of relief and Professor sat on the chair when he found her answering the question.

"The requirements to start trading in Stock Market are

Firstly, Open a Demat Account. All banks generally open Demat account free of charge and charge very nominally as yearly charges.

Secondly, arrange a broker and through broker you can start trading in stock market.

In case you don't want to trade offline and wants to do it yourself online, then you need to open an Online Trading account, get your Bank and Demat account attached. Then you can pick stock, transfer money to online broking account, purchase shares, sell shares and so on, its (insert 'between t & s) very simple. Companies like Sharekhan, Kotak securities, Keynote Capitals, ICICI Direct etc provide all these facilities."

Students were shocked once again at her answer and even Prof Shashank was amused. All were wondering how can she know so much about stock market trading, she was just a fresher in the college. Kapil said slowly to Vihaan, "Look I said, I saw her in BSE, so that means she also has some knowledge on it. That means she was there."

Prof. Shashank said, "Fantastic dear, you made my work easier" and he started explaining further.

He added, "Trading in secondary market happens through placing of orders by the investors and their matching with a counter order in the trading system. Orders refer to instructions provided by a customer to a brokerage firm, for buying or selling a security with specific conditions. These conditions may be related to the price of the security (limit order or market order or stop loss orders) or related to time (a day order or immediate or cancel order)."

Prof Shashank tried his level best to explain the concept however he was also very sure that they could understand only 60 % of what he said. He was mentally prepared to explain again when the time comes.

"OK Now Let us understand what is Money Market", said Professor.

He shared the slides:

Money Market

Instruments have a maturity period less than 1 year. Various Instruments under Money Market

Cash

Money that is lent for a short period of time like one day, one week or fortnight is known as Call Money or Notice Money. Participants: Banks/Financial Institution

Treasury Bills

They are negotiable securities issued by RBI and are highly liquid.

Tenure: 91 days or 364 days.

Commercial paper is a money market security issued by large banks and corporations. It is generally not used to finance long-term investments but rather for purchases of inventory or to manage working capital. It is commonly bought by money funds (the issuing amounts are often too high for individual investors), and is generally regarded as a very safe investment. As a relatively low risk option, commercial paper returns are not large. There are four basic kinds of commercial paper: promissory notes, drafts, checks, and certificates of deposit.

They are issued by only corporate who have a min net worth of 5 crores and have a safe investment rating from credit agency. They are debt instruments issued by companies to meet short-term financing needs. Higher ratings for these securities are P1-CRISIL, A1-ICRA.

Certificate of Deposits (C.D)

Money deposited in a bank or savings and loan for a stated time period and normally paying a fixed rate of interest.

A Certificate of deposit is s customized fixed deposit either with a bank or companies.

A certificate of deposit (CD) is a time deposit with a bank or Companies. CDs are generally issued by commercial banks but they can be bought through brokerages. They bear a specific maturity date (from three months to five years), a specified interest rate, and can be issued in any denomination, much like bonds.

A certificate of deposit is a promissory note issued by a bank. It is a time deposit that restricts holders from withdrawing funds on demand. Although it is still possible to withdraw the money, this action will often incur a penalty

CDs offer a slightly higher yield than T-Bills because of the slightly higher default risk for a bank but, overall, the likelihood that a large bank will go broke is pretty slim. Of course, the amount of interest you earn depends on a number of other factors such as the current interest rate environment, how much money you invest, the length of time and the particular bank you choose. While nearly every bank offers CDs, the rates are rarely competitive, so it's important to shop around.

Corporate bonds

They are issued by corporate and are generally unsecured and evidenced by a certificate issued by the company acknowledging the debt. They usually have a fixed coupon rate.

Government Securities

They are usually long term and secured government borrowings. They are also considered as Money market instruments because it can be bought and sold within a year. They are absolutely risk free and come with a fixed Coupon rate.

"The other ways are **Repos and Reverse Repos"** Prof. Shashank continued.

"**Repos** (or Repurchase agreements) are a very popular mode of short-term (usually overnight) borrowing and lending, used mainly by investors dealing in Government securities. The arrangement involves selling of a tranche of Government securities by the seller (a borrower of funds) to the buyer (the lender of funds), backed by an agreement that the borrower will repurchase the same at a future date (usually the next day) at an agreed price. The difference between the sale price and the repurchase price represents the yield to the buyer (lender of funds) for the period. Repos allow a borrower to use a financial security as collateral for a cash loan at a fixed rate of interest. Since Repo arrangements have T-bills as collaterals and are for a short maturity period, they virtually eliminate the credit risk.

Reverse repo is the mirror image of a repo, i.e., a repo for the borrower is a reverse repo for the lender. Here the buyer (the lender of funds) buys Government securities from the seller (a borrower of funds) agreeing to sell them at a specified higher price at a future date.

Professor supplied lot of data to work on and was satisfied with his effort. Suddenly a voice raised.

'"Sir, can you tell me, we often hear Repo rate and Reverse rates are been hiked and then we also see experts and TV anchors discussing the repercussions on Home loan, Education loan and inflation. How these things are related?" asked Nisaa.

And soon the bell rang.

But Professor Shashank preferred to reply her.

"See when there is excess of money in the market, it results into inflation as people are least bothered of valuation of anything. Therefore to curb inflation Govt increases Repo and Reverse Repo rate thus creating artificial money crunch/scarcity in the market. However it results in increase of interest on Loan, thus again reducing spending, which may result in reduction of inflation. But many times it has been seen that these efforts are inadequate as there are various other factors which are responsible for the inflation."

"I will discuss about the factors in next session, ok . . . That's all for the day, Thank u." Professor left the classroom saying goodbye to the students and with a cute and satisfied smile on his face. And students also paid him adieu by the corporate claps and they also left the classroom.

By the end of the lecture Sharon had become centre of attraction. Reason was partly her wild get up that has created sensation in the campus and secondly her mind blowing answers in the class. Sharon soon became a topic for hot discussion in the campus. She was keeping her things in her bag, meanwhile Kapil was waiting, with the hope perhaps she may notice him. But, alas!!! she didn't even notice him and left the classroom. Perhaps she had something else in her mind and that is Professor Shashank. Disappointed Kapil left the room and found Vihaan smiling at him. He said, "What???", making useless effort to hide his intentions. Vihaan said, "Nothing", though he understood what was going on in Kapil's mind, as this was not the first time, he had the tendency to fall for every girl, but this time he looked more serious.

As Sharon passed through the corridors to the canteen . . . she was stared by the boys . . . few hit the wall in attempt to look at her and got hurt . . . few, who were then busy with their girlfriend also got stuck by seeing Sharon . . . few started flirting her as she crossed the corridors . . . seemed as if she was being observed by whole campus . . . . Boys couldn't take their eyes off her due to her being the smartest, bold and most beautiful 'new' girl in the campus and girls couldn't cause they wanted to find out what boys looked in her. Perhaps it was her glam look, confident walk, attitude, innocent beauty and sharp brain and bold looks, which made her so special. When she walked, students automatically got aside to give her way . . . Sharon was aware of all these reactions, but these things were of least importance to her. She was least perturbed by such reactions, seemed she didn't even bother, without getting shy or disturbed or without noticing all these things, she went straight to the canteen where she found Prof. Shashank and went to him to ask something.

Kapil, Vihaan, Ashok, Chhabi, Nisaa also went to the canteen at the 'same place' and had few snacks with Kapil's all time favourite Madrasi coffee and Vihaan ordered for ice tea and others ordered for themselves as well.

After having something, as they were about to leave Chhabi passes a cute smile to Kapil, which as usual he ignored, because his current area of interest was Sharon. Suddenly, he found Sharon discussing something with Prof. Shashank. Sharon was asking something about stocks and derivatives. He went closer to hear them and found them discussing something about stocks, but was soon caught by the eyes of Sharon, and was caught red-handed. He got embarrassed, but was still feeling victorious as he got the attention of Sharon.

She just turned to leave and she saw Kapil. Kapil was quite sure that this time she will definitely say something, he also started moving towards her slowly throwing fingers on hair, playing with his HTC brand new cell phone, but alas!!! He was again disappointed and she, busy on her tab, crossed him unknowingly. But Kapil became more determined to include her in his fans list and left for home.

Ganpati Sthapana

And here arrived the day of colors, the day of 'Gannu' with great pomp and show . . . A big idol of Ganpati ji was brought on a 'rath' with loud music, students playing with colors, dancing, singing and enchanting the mantras of God Ganpati . . . . The voice and sounds filled the environment with such spiritualism that it seemed that the nature itself is welcoming God Ganpati, little drizzles also graced the occasion by their benign presence. Everyone was so excited and happiness was visible on their faces.

Now the idol was carried by four of the students and it was placed on the platform prepared for sthapana of Ganpatiji and now the voices were prominent . . . All the rituals followed by Aarti were performed. Loud prayers, ghanta, music, bells . . . . the whole environment was filled with the enchanting . . . students were playing with colors throwing on one another and enjoying the moment, . . . they repeated in excitement "Ganpatiji ki jai" . . . . "ek do teen chaar, ganpati ki jai jai kar, char paanch cheh saath, ganpati hamare saath". All the students and all the professors including Professor Shashank were part of the ritual.

All the students including Nisaa, Chhabi, Kapil, Ashok, Vihaan and Sharon were participating in the rituals and procedures, all were looking as if they were mobile idol of colors. Few were dancing along with Prof. Shashank, while Nisaa stood nearby. She was enjoying the dances by all, she clapped and laughed over the cartoon like dances of her colleagues and she also found Professor

Shashank enjoying it. Professor Shashank was dancing like a fire that ignites all the students. They danced and danced . . . Soon she found professor breathing heavily and he went on the chair to sit. He was feeling tired very badly. Nisaa went to him and offered water. He took it immediately and drank all. She just asked professor if he needed anything else. He replied, "I want to dance, more." And smiled and again joined the students.

On the other side, Sharon, in white chicken chudidar suit, was the only one, who managed to save herself from those colors. She didn't want to be the part of those worthless rituals but since her class mates and other students were present there, so she also thought to stand. Students at the back suddenly started throwing colors powder on one another and started putting them on each other's faces. Suddenly Sharon felt that few 'abeer' was on her hair, as soon as she put her fingers on parting-line of her hair, . . . she found red color on her fingers . . . . and in no time she just burst out and ran away from the temple. On the way she met Kapil, he tried to put color on her face, though she denied but still he wanted to do that, and "Chataakk" a big slap by Sharon. Kapil was shocked but he could clearly see her red eyes, water in her eyes were trickling down, but he got annoyed. He never expected this from his dream girl. It was like bolt from the blue, as if someone has awaken him up from his dreams. He raged in anger and left the place. Sharon in irritation ran as fast as she could and entered into a classroom and sat on her seat, but the chorus voices of "ek do teen chaar, ganpati ki jai jai kar, char paanch chah saath, ganpati hamare saath" accompanied by the music, ghanta, manjeera, all those sounds entered into her ears like a melted glass, she broke and started crying loudly, she ran and closed the doors and windows so that no voice should enter into her ears . . . . she put her hands on her ears. She was crying and crying . . . . She cursed the God . . . She did fight with Him . . . . She blamed Him for whatever has happened to her . . . . She just kept on abusing Him . . . . She was so much irritated by those enchants and mantras of praises for God . . . all this was unbearable for her . . . she was furious and frustrated at the foolishness, stupidity of humans who believe that the idol of clay can do anything, she felt pity for those who bow their heads, join their hands in front of an 'idol', she thought perhaps they don't know that God himself is helpless in front of the fate, if anything really exists is the destiny, which can be changed by only karma i.e actions that's it. Her belief was so firm that she couldn't even bear the enchanting and prayers. She felt as if, the one whom she hates most, his friends and classmates are bowing to him like the slaves and the followers. She felt as if He won again, she again was defeated, as if he was saying, "Look, this is my terror, no one can dare to forget me and challenge me. I am the God, I can do everything." And this is what she had decided will never do again . . . She will never bow in front of this so called God, whatever may be the consequences, she had decided that she will prove that God is nothing . . . . He is just an Idol . . . . perhaps it was her anger, frustration and irritation . . .

After an hour, when everything was quiet she came down again, tried to keep her normal composure and took whatever eatables 'prasad' were provided, with a little smile on her face.

She tried to find Kapil but couldn't. She was embarrassed and sorry for her behaviour. But this was the first time when Sharon was looking for Kapil and he was nowhere. Her eyes were red and sadness was

on her face, she was crying in heart but was looking for Kapil to ask for forgiveness. She sank because she knew why Kapil was not a part of the crowd. She turned back in despair and found Professor Shashank. She was surprised to see him there and just asked, "How r u, sir?"
"Am fine, n wat abt u?" replied professor in a thoughtful manner.

"Me too fine"

"So, looking for someone"

"a . . . a . . . no . . . no . . . sir not at all . . ."

"its ok . . . i understand. He will take some time to recover."

"Sir . . . ???? u . . ."

"Yes, i saw . . ."

"Am sorry, sir . . . its just happened . . . I didn't intend to do it. Sir, actually I want to confess something"

"Its ok dear . . . . i don't know what you have gone through or your story but am sure it's not gr8. You couldn't control your emotions but my suggestion is that running away from your problems will only enhance the pain and ache. I would suggest, face it right today, tomorrow is too late. Hope u understood wat em trying to say . . . God bless u . . ."

"Yes sir i got it, thank u so much sir . . ."

And they both dispersed.

A Walk through Stock Exchange

The students were waiting for Prof. Shashank. Kapil and Vihaan as usual were sitting on the second bench of middle row, Sharon on first bench of middle row and Chhabi on the second bench of third row, so that she can see Kapil properly and Nisaa on the first row. Sharon was quite restless and was thinking how to talk to Kapil. At the same time, she was busy on her tab doing something, though Kapil was annoyed with her but his eyes automatically went towards quiet Sharon and all he can observe was the red screen with some movements. He wasn't able to understand what does she always do on her tab. "What does she thinks of herself?" suddenly this thought came into his mind. Meanwhile enters Nisaa with the great news, "Hey, the Fresher's party has been scheduled on 21st September, 2013. Isn't it great!!! :p" Suddenly her eyes went to Sharon, thankfully she was busy in her own thoughts and on her tab, hence can't hear much. This news spread like wild fire in the campus. Everyone started discussing what to perform, with whom to perform, who shall be the partner, and above all who will be their partners for the ramp walk? And similar chaos was in the classroom as well.

And then enters Prof. Shashank in the classroom with his usual smile and gestures. Though it was not too cold, but still unlike professor was always in full sleeves and a half sleeved cardigan but he looked smart in that too. He was also now aware about the Fresher Party news and expected disturbance in the classroom, but was not at all perturbed by the same. He was capable of managing students and they welcomed him with corporate clap.

"Hmm . . . so got the news for fresher's?"

"Yes sir" in unison.

"Great, bt I expect it won't effect your attendance, right . . ."

"Yes sir, sure it won't . . ." many voices.

"Fine then, let's start." He went towards his bag, as he moved towards his bag suddenly a thought came into Sharon's mind "my chocolates" but professor again turned back, seemed as if he had forgotten something and looked a bit confused. And then he started the lecture with a discussion on stock markets.

"Sir, we often hear the word BSE, NSE how are these related to stock markets?", asked one of the students.

"Oh!! Wait . . . I will cm back to u soon."

Suddenly he remembered something and he again went towards his bag and yes there the professor took out a carry bag consisting of two Dairy Milk silks and with this there was a loud applause for a great professor and a brilliant student. Sharon was so glad to have those Dairy milk silk . . . her happiness was like a small kid. Everyone could see the happiness on her face . . . she was smiling . . . she said, "Thank u so much sir, i will study harder." "God bless" replied professor.

Then professor asked, "Yes someone asked something"

The student repeated again," Sir are BSE and NSE related to stock markets?"

But before Professor could answer, Sharon got up and Interrupted "They are Stock exchanges, you trade stocks there.".

"Perfect Sharon" said Prof Shashank proudly, "You are absolutely right. Actually these are the stock exchanges and besides these there are many other stock exchanges in different parts of the country . . . ."

Suddenly a beep sounded and there was a call for Sharon, she, like an obedient student, took permission from Prof. Shashank and went out of the classroom to attend the call. She was busy on her cell phone when Ashok arrived and was about to enter the classroom but was stopped by Prof. Shashank and he wasn't allowed to enter the classroom for being late. Disappointedly he went out of the classroom and kept his bag aside and sat on the floor, where suddenly he saw Sharon. The punishment, few minutes back which was like a curse to him, now proved to be a blessing. He immediately galloped towards her. Sharon just disconnected her call and she was suddenly stopped by Ashok.

"Hii, em Ashok . . . V r buddies for d same programme" said Ashok, offering for a handshake.

"Hii" said Sharon indifferently with a small smile and started moving towards classroom.

"Hey! Wait Wait"

"What??"

"Actually em late . . ."

"So"

"I need ur help, dear"

"What, help?"

"What is the topic that will be covered today in the lecture"

"Its abt BSE & NSE"

"Shitt man!! Oh yaar please help me, i have a little knowledge abt it n he wont allow me to attend his lecture . . . Only u can help me out . . . can u tell me something abt it . . ."

"Nooooo way, I cant miss his lecture"

"Oh cm on, wat r friends for? I know u r very intelligent. Plzz plzz for God's sake"

"uff . . . . Ohkk Ohkk . . . . I will help u. Happy now . . . !!!"

Sharon was a helpful person, she agreed though uninterestingly and asked him to come to canteen after the lecture, but he kept on insisting and she was left with no choice but to agree and went with him to canteen.

As usual canteen was full of students, bustling with all kinds of activities. As it was the most happening place in the campus which witnessed different love stories, clashes, arguments and celebrations', but today they were more busy in discussing fresher's party. As Ashok and Sharone entered, he could clearly see the admiration on the face of boys for Sharon, but she as usual was busy on her tab. They occupied a corner and then Ashok ordered for two cups of coffee and began discussing about the stock and exchanges. He was aware that he was with the most beautiful girl of the campus. He tried to see with the corner of his eyes, he was being observed by all the boys in the canteen. He was on top of the world.

Sharon started explaining "Stock exchanges are similar to any market. For example we go to Mall and there we purchase various types of goods with different rates. The mall gives us opportunity to purchase the available goods, we also negotiate for price. In same way Stock exchanges are nothing but place where seller and buyer come together, they negotiate on price and they purchase or sell their securities. But while doing that since the exchange, the place has provided seller and buyer to come together, the stock exchanges charges nominal charges which are known as brokerage collected by the brokers who act as mediators between seller and buyer of the security."

Ashok said "You know lot of things, can you tell me which are the prominent exchanges in India and speciality of them?"

Sharon said "Why not, let me tell you about two important Stock exchanges of India, they are NSE (National Stock exchange) and BSE (Bombay Stock exchange)".

Sharon was excited as someone was asking her about something which she was passionate about. She started explaining and Ashok started jotting down the points in his notebook.

The **National Stock Exchange (NSE)** is the India's largest securities exchange in terms of daily trade numbers. It offers automated trading of variety of securities, including equity, corporate debt, central and state government securities, commercial papers, exchange traded funds. The exchange has more than

1000 listed members. NSE specialises in three market segments like wholesale debt, capital market and Futures & Options. NSE started operations in 1984. NSE also set up as index services firm known as India Index services and Products limited (IISL) and has launched several stock indices like S&P CNC Nifty, CNX Nifty Junior, CNX 100, S&P CNX 500, CNX midcap.

The **Bombay Stock Exchange (BSE)** dates back to 1875. It was organised under the name of "The Native Stock and Share Brokers Association" as a voluntary and non profit making association. This premier stock exchange is the oldest stock exchange in Asia.

The BSE has over 6000 stocks listed, it enumerates for more than two-third of the total trading volume in India. Since establishment it has played avital role in the growth of capital market in Inida. It makes use of BSE Sensex which is an index of 30 big and developed stocks. The index provides an evaluation the comprehensive performance of BSE and is very much traded throughout the world.

Ashok was just listening to her continuously . . . and was astonished by her knowledge. He could not believe such an intelligence behind a beautiful face. "Beauty with brains!!!" the only thought came in his mind.

And then there was bell which started ringing. The Class was over. Professor Shashank came out of the class room and he saw Sharon with Ashok. Sharon felt guilty and avoided eye contact with Professor. She abused Ashok in her heart as he was the culprit cause of which she had to miss Prof Shashank's lecture.

She excused Ashok for a while and in no time as soon as the professor left, she rushed into the classroom, took out the chocolates and distributed it to all the students. Kapil had mixed emotions, was glad but at the same time he was angry and so he didn't said anything, rest of the students congratulated her. Sharon saw Kapil and she knew why he didn't say anything, was still feeling guilty for what had happened and decided to sort out this anyhow. Few of the seniors were jealous and didn't take the chocolate but in this way she was able to build a rapport with all. She shared her victory with all. This was something which Kapil liked most. Sharon was always taken as a self centred girl but today she changed that opinion. Though she wanted to share it with professor also but due to bunking the lecture she couldn't muster enough courage to go and meet him.

Then Sharon came back to Ashok, gave him also a bite of chocolate. Ashok congratulated her, he was awed by the way Sharon explained him the stock exchange, BSE and NSE. He was wondering how can she know so much about the exchange. He was literally in love for the knowledge she possesses.

He asked her questions after questions and she was answering him. The coffee was over but he wanted to know more about the stocks and that too from Sharon. Finally with great courage he said "Sharon can we meet at Park Avenue for dinner" and before she could say anything Ashok said "It's not a date but i just want to know more about the stocks".

It was the first time that Sharon was a bit moved though she soon relaxed by the second line said by

Ashok and said" Fine, sharp at 7 pm. Park Avenue" Even though it charges slightly more but allows client to stay there for hours and hours without any interruption. The joint had become a famous place for Business meetings and Lovers spot. With this promise, both of them were about to leave the canteen.

As they were about to leave suddenly Ashok, without thinking for a while, asked Sharon," Will you become my partner for the ramp walk?" Sharon straight away, within a moment, replied, "No". Her reply was so firm that Ashok couldn't manage to ask her again. Being the talk of the town, it was a big question for all, who will be the person with Sharon will do the ramp walk and if not then why not? Many of them even tried to be in her friends' list on Facebook, but Sharon was very choosy about accepting friends' requests, hence only few lucky ones, could manage to do so . . . and Kapil and Ashok were amongst those lucky ones . . .

By now most of the students had left except Kapil, who was still in the canteen. Sharon, while keeping her things back, suddenly saw him . . . and then suddenly Ashok's question arose a thought in Sharon's mind as well and she got an idea, which was again a secret for all like her. She looked at Kapil, smiled and walked towards him. She started, "Hii" (Sharon had an idea when she saw Ashok as she remembered his request to her)

" . . . ."

"May I, sit here? . . ."

"As you wish . . ."

"Em really extremely sorry for dat day . . . . it was not for you . . . i mean it was something else, u just came in the way, dats it . . . ." "Em really very very sorry for dat"

"Its k, I have to go, now . . ." said Kapil and left without bothering about her.

"But . . . ." Sharon couldn't complete her sentence. She had no option left than to leave for her home as well.

After parting with Sharon, Ashok went straight to Crossword and started searching for books on stock market. He did not want to belittle himself when he would be discussing the stocks with Sharon in the evening.

He asked the Manager" Which is the best and the simplest book, which will give me knowledge in one hour". The Manager laughed and said, i don't know whether you can grasp about the Stock market in one hour, but yes i can certainly suggest you few books which deals with the basics".

Based on the recommendations, Ashok grabbed few books and ran home. He had very limited time and had to give good impression as today was his Date even though it was one sided. He started reading the book.

'The Flop Date'

Ashok reached Park Avenue an hour before with Note Pad and couple of pens and pencils. He waited and alas she was there, exactly at 7 pm. He had booked the table and had planned out what he would order etc.

Ashok said "Thanks for coming, Sharon. What would you like to have to start with juice, soup . . .". Sharon said "Anything, but let's get on with the work. You wanted to know more about Stocks, so shoot, I will answer whatever i know, if anything is missing, we shall get it verified by Prof Shashank."

Ashok was slightly disappointed, yes he wanted to know about stocks but was also very eager to have some general talks with Sharon. She had become an apple of his eye not because of her knowledge but also because of her looks. He had gone flat on her but to keep (the) conversation going he had to discuss stocks.

Ashok said "Can you tell me what are the types of shares?" Sharon said there are types of shares like Preferential Shares, Equity Shares etc. But the commonly shares which we talk about loosly and trade on stock market are equity shares. She showed him the book.

We mainly have Equity shares and Prefernce shares. The Preference shares has certain preference over equity shares on terms of dividend payements and claim incase the company is wound up. However they don't have equivalent voting rights as the common stock holder has.

"So, are the preference shares redeemable?" asked Ashok.

"In India, preference shares are redeemable (callable by issuing firm) and preference dividends are cumulative. By cumulative dividends, we mean that in case the preference dividend remains unpaid in a particular year, it gets accumulated and the company has the obligation to pay the accrued dividend and current year's dividend to preferred stockholders before it can distribute dividends to the equity shareholders. An additional feature of preferred stock in India is that during such time as the preference dividend remains unpaid, preference shareholders enjoy all the rights (e.g. voting rights) enjoyed by the common equity shareholders. Some companies also issue convertible preference shares which get converted to common equity shares in future at some specified conversion ratio. In addition to the equity and fixed-income markets, the derivatives market is one of India's largest and most liquid."

The Discussion was going on smoothly. They had their Dinner, Stock was at the centre stage of discussion but they also talked about each other's hobbies, friends and so many other things.

Finally the clock struck 10:30 pm then Sharon asked "I need to go now.". "Ok as u wish, by the way how did u come, if u won't mind can i drop you" replied Ashok. Sharon said "I have come by auto but sure if u don't have any problem, you can drop me at my place."

Ashok was on 9th cloud, his whole day's preparation, prayers were to be fulfilled . . . .

He was so excited that he didn't bother to check whether his motorcycle's petrol tank had any fuel. The bike was running at brisk speed and suddenly it slowed down and stopped instantly.

Ashok realized what he has done, it was so embarrassing, the whole effort was going to be futile and in vain just cause of his little stupid carelessness. But it is said that whatever is destined to happen will happen.

On the other hand, Sharon was cool and realising that Ashok is embarrassed, she asked him to be relaxed and said that she can manage. Sharon's house was still 5 km from the place and the vehicle was not starting not even by the choke. Finally Ashok had to accept the fact that the 'date' was ruined. He then suggested Sharon to take an auto and go back to her house. Which she readily accepted . . .

10:00 a.m., Wednesday, 18th September, 2013

'Ganpati Visarjan'

Kapil was still annoyed with Sharon, and he did not even try to see her in the last few days. She attended the 'Arti' for all the five days . . . . Perhaps she agreed to the professor's advice and realized that it's better to fight the enemy from face to face and not by running away. So, everyday she came for the Arti and everyday she looked into the eyes of God, made fun with her colleagues, laughed a lot, cracked jokes . . . She tried her best to overcome her weakness and to some extent she was successful. Her eyes were trying to see Kapil but he avoided her completely. She had decided that she will ask him to pardon her. Though he was now more curious to know about her, but he was annoyed and angry that how can she slap him.? Perhaps his ego was hurt. It was just a coincidence that Kapil was the only one who saw that Sharon, when she was completely different from her usual attitude, perhaps this was the actual Sharon, who always fights with her to overcome her weaknesses, who shows herself to be strong, who try to betray others, sometimes even herself also . . . . but now her reality was in front of Kapil.

Today was the Ganpati visarjan and like always it started with the Arti and all the students were present in the arti. There was a 'rath' which was used to take Ganpati murti from campus to the place where it is immersed. A loud music with songs of Ganpati bappa mourya has filled the environment with spirituality. Prof. Shashank who was called as the best entertainer amongst his colleagues, also participated in the activities enthusiastically. He is strict in the lecture room, but outside the class he is known to be the best friend, a jolly good person, who loved fun and frolics and that is why he is a favourite teacher of all students. Sharon was also a part of this ritual, she was enjoying the music and her body was ready to move with the rhythm but she forced herself and decided not to. She along with Kapil, Ashok, Chhabi, Nisaa, Vihaan . . . . also participated in the ceremony. Though for Sharon it was just an attendance but for many it was like Ganpatiji was again going back and they were sad and some even cried . . . Sharon was really surprised to see this, how can one be so attached to just an idol . . .

The procession started moving towards the river, with big bang dance, music all were in a dancing mode, they danced enchanted "ek do teen char, Ganpati ki jai jai kaar, char paanch chheh saat, ganpati hamare saath" . . . . they all including Prof. Shashank, students did dancing, singing reached to the river and the idol was being immersed in the water with big enchanting and prayers . . . .

Everyone prayed for the good luck and asked 'Ganuu' to come next year soon . . . . All became emotional while bidding adieu to Lord Ganpati . . . .

The possession started returning and Sharon was thinking "How to talk to Kapil, how to call him, how to start, what to say, what not to say . . . . so many thoughts came in her mind in those few seconds". Suddenly she became firm and went directly to Kapil. Kapil was with his friends.

She went there and said to Kapil "I want to talk to u". Kapil couldn't say her no in front of his friends, so he came near to Sharon and said, "What?".

Sharon hesitated, but said, "Please forgive me. Please try to understand me . . . .". Kapil was quiet taken aback and he didn't utter a single word. Sharon again said, "Please forgive me." Kapil didn't said anything and left. Sharone kept on requesting him but his ears became deaf to her request. Sharon was hurt, her eyes became moist her face reddened and she couldn't help herself, tears rolled down from her eyes. She was noticed by Nisaa. Nisaa took her to her room, when she found her in such situation.

Listening to him carefully and silently, Saloni was amused by the moment . . . Perhaps she was imagining herself with all the characters. Suddenly Prof Ranade realised that this is the first time when he was continuously speaking on and Saloni was silent, unlike her nature.

Suddenly they were interrupted by the air-hostess as they were offered drinks and snacks . . . there was option for cocktails and mocktails as well. Seeing which Saloni got excited and wanted to go for cocktail but looking at Prof. Ranade, she controlled her feelings and softly ordered for one orange juice. Professor ordered one ice tea for himself . . .

They started enjoying their drink . . . Saloni was silently sipping hers and professor as well, perhaps both were in deep contemplation of their thoughts. Suddenly professor realised that Saloni was also very quiet, perhaps he got habitual to her continuous talks and her silence made him uneasy. He just tried to look at her with the corner of his eye. This time he saw her from very close distance . . . . She was neither fair nor dark . . . . Her name complemented her complexion, her few brown strands of hair were still disturbing her but this time she didn't put them aside as if she gave them permission to touch her face and even her lips, her soft lips which became wet as soon as the juice touched her lips, which she licked through her tongue, to clean. Professor felt as its long he has observed anyone so minutely and so closely. Suddenly he took his eyes off and drowned in his own thoughts, it reminded him of his past when he had rejected his love. Saloni reminded him of his love, his dream, his passion, his habit, his addiction, 'Anamika'. As soon as he finished his drink, he found Saloni glancing at her, he said, "What?". She replied, "What happened next?", of course she was talking about the story . . . . he smiled and started from where he left . . .

Nisaa's Room at Beta Hostel

Best Friends . . . .

Nisaa took Sharon to her room that was in Beta Hostel. She gave her water to drink and few snacks. Nisaa didn't know anything, but she didn't initiate the talk, she wanted Sharon to empty her heart out. She was unaware of the truth she was about to encounter.

As soon as Nisaa asked her what happened, "Sharon started sobbing . . ."

Nisaa was expecting some outrage but this was different. Sharon was crying sitting in front of her. Nisaa was not able to understand that what had made her cry. She tried to console Sharon and also asked her what happened. Sharon was crying, her eyes were continuously supporting her to stimulate her emotions in the form of her tears.

Nisaa was completely blank, anyone in place of her would have been blank because no one knew the darker side of Sharon. The darker nights she had passed, the pain she had stored in her heart, the loneliness she had felt in her life, the bitter truth she had tasted, the words she heard which hurt her . . . no one knew that Sharon which seemed to be very hot, bold, arrogant, proud and filled with attitude, was in reality battered by destiny, who also had similar desires, feelings like all girls . . . she is no different from all, it's her life that has made her so . . . . no one knew that every day after going back from college she spends her evening in isolation and fights with someone who left her, fights with her destiny, fights

54

with God that he was unable to change her destiny . . . she cries and sobs with her only companion, her 'Teddy' which was gifted to her by a very special person of her life, her man, her best half, her husband. Hours n hours she spent with her teddy, writing poems for her beloved . . . sometimes despair sometimes hope . . . and her evening is spent in this confusion. Everyday she dreams of her beloved and wakes up with new hope, energy and enthusiasm, perhaps every night he comes to give her strength and confidence to tell her that she is capable of changing the world alone and she gets manipulated by his talks thinking that "Yes. If my Viraat, said so, i can do it."

Nisaa gave her another glass of water, Sharon became a bit normal . . . . Nisaa asked her again, "What has happened?"

Sharon narrated," I never wanted to do this and now he is not forgiving me, he does not want to listen to me. I don't want to hurt anyone and you know i have very few friends, i don't want to lose one more person."

"One more person??? What do you mean?" said Nisaa.

Sharon told her everything which she had in her heart. She just poured out her heart in front of Nisaa. Nisaa was surprised and stunned to hear the story, she was in dead shock. She was unaware of this side of cool and jazz looking Sharon. She took a sip of water and said, "I am proud of you, Sharon. You have proved that girls are no more dependent on someone and they are capable of taking care of themselves. And don't worry about Kapil, he is very good at heart. He will forgive you soon . . . ., relax dear . . ." Nisaa gave her a tight hug and kissed on her forehead. Sharon felt so safe, light and warmth in her arms that she remained in her arms for a minute. After all Nisaa was the first person in the college with whom she had confided her life story. Sharon was now feeling better and was ready for the next day, she left for the day.

After Sharon left, Nisaa made a call to Kapil to tell him that Sharon is not fine and she is really sorry for what had happened.

"Hello, whose is this?" a heavy voice, though it was Kapil but due to sleep, it sounded so.

"Hii"

"Yes, who?"

"Stupid this is me . . . Nisaa."

"Oh, Nisaa . . . . hii hw r u? Anything important? . . ."

"Yes, it's about Sharon"

"Oh.!! What's dat??" Suddenly his voice became normal and conscious."

"Just want to tell you that she is not fine and she is really sorry for her act . . . literally she was crying just because you didn't forgive her . . ." Nisaa said in authoritative voice.

"Oh . . . really did she tell you what she did?"

"Yes she did, and she also told me that she didn't do that intentionally, it was her own personal reasons why she got upset on that day, now i request you to please forgive her. Look this is something really very serious. Many a times what we see is far different from the truth."

"Oh . . . so she is using you for this . . ."

"Oh cm on . . . please, she don't even know dat i have called you. Now look Kaps, if u trust me, you have to forgive her. got it . . . cm on . . . don't give so much of attitude . . . K."

"Ok . . . bt if she will approach me one more time, then i will do it."

"Uff . . . . Ohkk baba, now go n sleep . . . bbyee"

"Byee"

Love Equations—In progress

Where everyone was thinking about the partner, Vihaan had already chosen one, of course it was Chhabi. Though Chhabi was not interested in Vihaan but being a friend she couldn't say no to him, to be the partner in ramp walk with him . . . . and along with that she was also a good singer so they also decided to perform a duet song.

During the college hours they had no time to practice as Chhabi was more busier in observing Kapil than to concentrate on her performance "with Vihaan". So they decided to go somewhere outside for practice.

Finally they decided that near their college, was a small hill, an ideal place to practice. Chhabi also readily accepted because she always wanted to go there, she liked trekking and 'tila' was always in her list of favourite destination. "It would be a great place to practice," Chhabi told herself.

It was Thursday, they bunked their lectures and early in the morning at 8:00 a.m. they gathered near the tila. Chhabi, in a grey t-shirt, jeans, sports shoes, looked very young and cute . . . This was the first time Vihaan saw her in jeans, because generally she usually prefered salwar chudidar to jeans. But he was happy to see her and even complimented "U r lookin gr8 today". Chhabi gave smile with a blush. They started to climb the mountain. It was not too tough to climb it but still Vihaan held

Chhabi's hand to help her to climb the mountain. And in just 45 minutes, they were on the top of the 'tila'. Vihaan was still holding her hand. Chhabi said in a notorious voice with a witty smile, "Wanna still hold my hand?" Listening this Vihaan left her hand, actually he got a bit embarrassed but at the same time he was glad that at such a beautiful place, he is with Chhabi. Chhabi and Vihaan both were enchanted by the mesmerizing beauty of the tila. It was bright sun below, but a cool breeze on the tila, all over fresh green grasses, trees, surrounded by flowers, grazed by few of the sheeps and shepherds were sitting there, the scenic view of tila seemed as if they have reached the heaven.

For a moment they both felt as if, they were in a different world. A world far away from the mechanised world of materials. They sat on the grass for few minutes to enjoy the beauty, the smell of the fresh air, that filled them with a freshness.

Soon they started discussing about the song they will choose for duet song performance. Chhabi suggested few, Vihaan also suggested few and at last they finalized the song, "Suraj hua maddham" from Kabhi Khushi Kabhi Gum. Vihaan immediately downloaded the song from the net in his iphone. Both started listening to the song and tried to remember the lyrics . . . Chhabi also transferred to her cell phone through Bluetooth. Both used their earphones to listen to the song and started practising.

Chhabi started singing . . . She was in a perfect scale and tone . . . She was blessed with a very sweet voice and her melodious voice became more sweeter when she started singing the song. On listening to her song, Vihaan was hypnotized, he was so impressed by her magical voice, that he came near to Chhabi and held her hand, said," You sing great Chhabi . . . u r really a wonderful singer "and he took her face in cup of his hands and kissed on her forehead. This moment was like an electric current to Chhabi . . . she was stunned, her brains got numbed . . . she felt the shiver in her body as soon as Vihaan touched her and 'Kissed', she was just not able to recollect herself from sudden shock which she got, for a moment she couldn't even react . . . She felt so shy that she blushed . . . Her fair face was now pink and her eyes looked downwards which she was not able to raise, her heart beat faster and in a meek voice and with a little smile she said, "Thanks", perhaps her facial expression made Vihaan realize that he has done 'something'. But he didn't feel he did anything wrong and was sure that Chhabi will also feel the same . . . and to some extent he was right . . . and they both practised the song.

On the other hand Sharon had called Kapil in the college canteen to meet him. Kapil knew why she had called but he pretended as if he didn't know anything.

Both arrived at the college canteen at approx same time.

Sharon has reserved a chair for him. Both sat on the chair.

"Hi" Sharon initiated the talk.

"Hii, How are you?"

"Yeah am fine thanks, by the way wat wud you like to have cold or hot?"

"As you wish"

"Okzz . . . so cold coffee?" Kapil nodded in agreement. Sharon ordered two cold coffees with one plate momos.

"Kapil, you know why I have called you . . . i really em sorry for my act and if you want to punish me, you can do even that . . ."

"Its okk . . . i don't have any grudge against you . . . and i understand."

There order was now served. They had cold coffee and momos.

"So, really you have forgiven me . . . ." Sharon in an excited voice.

"Oh yes, come on am not Hitler . . ."

"Pakka . . ."

"Yes, dear, of course now what shall i do to assure you for the same . . ."

"A . . . . a . . . wud u be my partner for the ramp walk???"

"Wat? R u mad? Seniors and juniors ramp walk is not allowed . . . you will be disqualified from any of the contests . . . . no i can't . . ."

"No, u hv to else i won't do ramp walk . . . . you have to do if you have forgiven me . . . . plzzzz . . . . plzzzz"

"Ohkk . . . ohkkkk . . . u r really very stubborn"

"Thank you soooo much . . . ." Sharon was smiling like a kid.

By this time they had finished their coffee and momos as well and they both left for their respective lectures. Now they were friends.

Love in the air

It was the last day before Fresher's party. Everyone in the college was busy with their partners . . . some were preparing for the dances, some for skits, some making preparations for ramp walk. Sharon and Kapil also practised though no one knew about it. Now Vihaan and Chhabi were good friends . . . . silently only but Chhabi has also accepted his friendship . . .

They were in their classroom as it was empty and their practise was also going well, it was just Vihaan who sometimes, started doing masti and in fun he misses few of the 'sur' in song. Chhabi had to control him again and again to make him sit quietly and do practise. It was completely different experience for her. Vihaan, who is known for his silent nature, was completely changed person in front of her. This Vihaan was so humorous, funny, extrovert, talkative and who knows to express his feelings. Whatever may be the reason but she was happy with him. She liked his company.

She said, "Look Vihaan, please be serious, i want this performance to be best"

"Ok, What will i get if i will make a rocking performance?" Vihaan said.

"Whatever u will ask for"

"Pakka na . . . Don't forget your promise . . ."

"Sure, done . . ."

"Now just wait and watch" "We will be the best. \m/" and smiled.

Similar feeling was with Vihaan, he never knew that Chhabi, who is generally called as 'Bharat Mata' by her colleagues, can be so cool and bold. He was experiencing a new Chhabi who is sweet, sour, salty, bold, shy . . . in short a complete package . . . She is a beauty with brains as well . . . . which is generally a rare combination. He thought she has all the qualities of a good girl friend . . . . and smiled . . .

Chhabi who was observing him, asked the reason behind his smile . . . He replied, "I was thinking of hugging you."

"What??" annoyed Chhabi said and ran towards him to beat him . . .

Vihaan also started running and Chhabi followed Vihaan . . . . and they ran and ran, unless Vihaan was hit by a chair and he fall on a bench and Chhabi also fell on him . . . Chhabi tried to balance herself but all in vain . . . and in no time she was in the arms of Vihaan . . . . her hair flowing on his face . . . . She was so close to Vihaan that he can easily feel her warm breath, her fast heart beat . . . . her glowing face was just a inch far away . . . her earlobes with a dangling earring were making Vihaan mad . . . he had extreme desire to kiss her but Chhabi was so shy that it was clearly visible on her face . . . her lips were shivering . . . . eyes were closed . . . . just hands were making useless efforts. Watching that he helped her to get up and so was she . . .

To lighten the situation, Vihaan tried to humour and said, "And it's done"

Anyhow balancing her, she stood shyly, putting her hair behind her ears, cleaning her clothes and asked," What?"

"HUG!!!"

"Awe . . . . UUUUUU . . . . I hate you . . ." annoyed Chhabi started going away from him.

"I m sorry, I m sorry!!! I m sorry ok., . . . i will not hug u . . . anymore." he said.

"Pakka na"

"Yup sure"

"Okk"

"Yes, i will not hug u anymore, but . . . ."

"But what??"

"But"

"But . . . ., will kiss u . . ." and he ran away.

This time Chhabi also smiled on his childish act . . . .

Freshers' Party—The most awaited moment

And here came the sparkling night when all the stars were gathered at one place and every girl was a princess and every boy was a prince charming. The college was decorated with lights . . . the college was transformed into a disco . . . light effects, loud music, surrounded by beautiful and hot babes and dude's it was really an alluring environment where no one can stay away from its effect.

All the seniors including Kapil, Ashok, Nissa, Vihaan, Chhabi were busy in the arrangement and looked after the participants, helping them to get ready for the show. Some were busy in photography, some on stage arrangement, some behind the stage, some for the dinner arrangements, some for the lighting etc. Sharon also helped the seniors in their task.

And here starts the show with a ramp walk where all the beauties were accompanied by the most handsome guys, who rocked the floor by their ramp walks and performance. The environment was filled by claps, background music, hooting on couples, whistles. After the ramp walk of all the juniors in which near about ten couples crossed the floor and then came the next couple, to the great surprise of all. Suddenly there was a silence, they were not able to believe and it was Sharon-Kapil together on the stage. A silence was followed by a huge clap and here was a most beautiful lady with the toughest hunk of the campus together on the floor and they ignited the show with their seducing gestures and appearance. Sharon was looking gorgeous in her round neck sheer blue lace gown with a jumpsuit underneath, the full sleeve floor length lace gown gave her a stylish look. Her face was glowing with a nude make-up, an eyeliner on her eyes, light kajal, with a light blue eye shadow gave her eyes a smoky look, a little rouse on cheeks and chin and tangerine red color lipstick that added to her grace and her brown wavy hairs, who were really well trained, played their role beautifully by floating on her neck and shoulders. She looked damn hot and beautiful. Kapil was also one of the most desirable guy and in his attire he was also looking most handsome in his carelessly tucked white shirt, black denim jacket accompanied by levies blue jeans with the white black striped belt and white and black checked scarf in the neck along with his goggles was a perfect look. And besides their dresses, Kapil and Sharon' s gestures, expression, body language, coordination, all were just awesome. And they left the floor with a few grand claps and admiration. Ashok was quite jealous of Kapil and annoyed with Sharon because she rejected his proposal. And the next couple was Chhabi and Vihaan . . . like always Chhabi was looking a hot chic in her bright red striped V-neck dress accompanied by her cream nude peep-toes gave her a complete babes look. In the same way Vihaan too was looking glamerous in his white shirt, black waist coat, black patiyala with hariyanvi slippers. Last but not the least were Ashok and Nisaa, where Nisaa was in black colored net saree, Ashok was in a dabang style and they both went passing through the ramp reminded of Salman Khan and Sonkashi Sinha in Dabangg. In this way, the first round of ramp walk was over.

Now was the time for different performances and here came Chhabi in yellow saree and Vihaan in yellow shirt and jeans, on the stage for their duet song performance . . . and the karaoke was played and they started singing "Suraj hua Maddham" . . . the whole environment was spellbound . . . their voices were echoing in the air and people were charmed by their song, besides the tune, they were able to coordinate properly, perhaps they felt the song and sang by looking into each other's eyes. As they ended, the arena was filled with a loud clap for continuously for few seconds . . . every one admired their performance. Similarly many more performances were done and last was the selection of Mr and Ms Freshers Octave 2k13 and two of the juniors were selected for the same and many more awards like Best

Attitude Male, Best Attitude Female, Best Smile, Best Get up and many other awards were given to the first semester students. All the faculties along with Professor Shashank also congratulated all the winners.

The programme was over and now it was the time for DJ and DJ Suketu was in the campus to rock the floor and it started with a big bang. Sharon and Kapil moved towards the first floor to drink water, Ashok also followed them, when they reached the first floor, suddenly Ashok came in front of them, Sharon was surprised to see him there and she asked, "Yes, Ashok. How come you are here?". Ashok made a witty smile and said, "Am sorry, if I disturbed you." "What do you mean?" Sharon said in an innocent voice. This time Ashok looked at Kapil and said in a taunting manner, "Pat gayi kya, Marle tu bhi chance pe dance mar le". Sharon understood what he was trying to say, before Kapil could say anything, Sharon immediately warned Ashok and said, "Hello, that's none of your business and better you mind your own language, or else you watch . . ." Ashok was embarrassed to see such a hyper reaction of Sharon and left. Kapil was also shocked to see this aspect of Sharon. Everyday he came to know something new about Sharon. He thought she was the one who never paid heed to me, she was the one who slapped me, she is the one who said sorry to me, she is the one who herself took initiative to ask me for being her partner in ramp walk and now she is the one who can scold anyone who tries to disrespect her or put fingers on her character. He was really impressed by the multi shaded personality of Sharon.

Thinking about Sharon, he didn't realize when they reached the DJ floor. And then started the heart throbbing dance, everyone including Kapil, Sharon, Ashok, Nisaa and others, rocked the floor through their electrifying dance. Sharon danced with Kapil and he was very happy, but Sharon was such a good dancer that he cannot catch her pace. She danced continuously without getting tired. All just enjoyed the dance and had lots of fun.

While everyone was busy on the dance floor Vihaan reminded Chhabi of the promise she gave, she could hardly listen to him in the loud music of DJ. So, Vihaan held her hand and took Chhabi on the terrace of the college building, where least sound was audible. Terrace was lightened by the glow of lights fitted across as if he stars have been scattered on the floors. It was so beautiful that for a second Vihaan also forgot why was he here. They both admired the beauty of that night, they sensed that this was not going to be a normal one for them. Suddenly Chhabi regaining her senses, hitting him from her elbow, asked Vihaan, "Are you nuts? What are we doing here? Look below is a DJ, we should be there, Why the hell you brought me here?" She kept on yelling. Then Vihaan said calmly, "You promised me something."

Chhabi said, "What?"

"You promised me that if I shall perform well, you will give me whatever i will ask for, right . . ."

"Ohh!! Yes"

"So now since I have performed well, so I want my gift . . ."

"Ohh really, who said you performed well?"

"Your eyes said . . ." Vihaan moved closer to Chhabi.

She became a bit uncomfortable, dropping her eye lashes, she said softly," Well . . . . Okk . . . . then you may ask your gift anytime. But now we are supposed to be there in the DJ"

"No, I want my gift now . . ."

Chhabi's heart began to beat faster, because her intuition said that Vihaan is not going to ask something so easy. She said softly, "O H K wats that? What gift do you want?"

This time Vihaan came very close to Chhabi . . . he tried to look into the eyes of Chhabi, though Chhabi again and again tried to divert her eyes off his face by looking here and there. When she tried to ignore him, he just put his arms across her waist. In nervousness, Chhabi got struck on a wall at the back due to which her saree got loosened. Her hair clip tried to disturb her, but Vihaan put off her clip and threw it aside. Now her hair was cuddling with her cute face, chins, cheeks and her shoulders. Vihaan asked, "Do you know what I want?"

She said, "No" though she could sense it.

Vihaan now tightly held her in his arms and their body can feel the warmth and touch of both. Vihaan again asked her the same question, and she again said no. Vihaan came more closer, this time his face was just in front of hers that her hair could touch his face also. Chhabi was breathing heavily, Vihaan can feel her breath.

Chhabi's heart was beating faster, Vihaan could listen to it . . . Her lips were shivering, eyes were closed and now she was completely in the circle of his arms. He gazed at her face for seconds and then silently said, "I love you so much. Do you?". Chhabi opened her eyes to see the face of her prince charming. She found him staring at her and she blushed. They stared at each other's eyes, beamed at each another, and in reply Chabbi just smiled and nodded her head and soon she was in his arms and then Vihaan expressed his gift, now Chhabi knew what was that and she gave him a silent permission and in no time Vihaan's hot lips were on Chhabi's soft lips. That was a passionate and sensuous one where tongues of both gave way to both, politely and gently cuddling with one another's. Vihaan's lips sucking hers and Chhabi's sucks Vihaan's. Vihaan held her tightly through waist, Chhabi took side of the wall and Vihaan slowly took her fingers to the back of her blouse and slowly untied the knots and kissed her on her back, making way out of her hair he kept on kissing her back, ears, eyes, cheek, chin, neck and below. He slowly slid off her blouse and kissed her on her shoulders. Chhabi shadowed her face through her palm in shyness and turned towards the wall, perhaps her shyness ignites the fire in Vihaan. He slowly removed his shirt and vest and went more closer to Chhabi, he turned her towards him and kissed her harder, a smooch, for a bit longer, Chhabi also kissed him harder, then on his neck, chest and then they went on and on and Vihaan and Chhabi both were drowned in the passion of their love that they forgot that they were supposed to go for the DJ down.

. . . .

No one knew that the night of shooting stars will suddenly convert into night of havoc. The DJ continued till 1:00 p.m._most of the faculties have left except two or three male faculties including Prof. Shashank. The DJ was followed by the dinner . . . but while dancing few of the seniors had liquor and few juniors also had . . . due to which many of them lost their control, some started shouting, some started abusing, some even said hard words about their relationship status as well . . . They started fighting and beating one another, In between one of the junior student threw a liquor bottle on a senior due to which his head started bleeding and this caused the seniors to hyper and since they were not able to see that junior student, they started beating all the junior students. Seeing this all the professors sent all the girls to the hostel. But the seniors and juniors had started a fight, some even brought hockey sticks from the gym and they started beating one another the fighting lasts for half an hour . . . . though professors were there but it started so suddenly that no one was able to control.

The fight had now reached on streets. The street from college to the main bazaar was with all students roaming in groups. It was as if civil war had started. In total more than 500 students were on streets moving in groups searching for their counterpart to take revenge. Professor Shashank took his bullet and few other Professors in their vehicle were moving on roads asking students to calm down, it took almost 2 hrs to get all students back to barracks. It was as if a civil commotion was averted. Meanwhile the Police party came honking and as usual to show their strength and power wanted to pickup students but Prof Shashank got in between and with his contacts with senior Police Officers could convince them that nothing had happened they would manage the whole thing internally.

Even though the whole episode ended but the arena which was looking pleasant a few minutes back, looked like a battling ground. All the students present were suspended for one week, with immediate action.

But that wasn't the solution, still lot of students kept grudges against each other and it had to be resolved.

Patch up at Dalal Street

The students gathered in the classroom. Professor had especially mailed each and every student from the first semester and second semester as well to be present for his special lecture on time. Students were curious to know after all what he was going to teach them for which he had mailed everyone to give attendance. They all were curiously waiting for the professor, though there was a silence in the environment due to the fresher's night incident. Suddenly entered the professor in the class with his usual smile and energy, and he directed all the students towards the door. Everyone started murmuring but they preferred to follow him than to ask. And he pointed them towards a bus, which was standing outside the gate of their college.

As soon as students saw the bus, they shouted aloud, as now they knew that they all are going for a trip and suddenly their confused faces were glowing with the happiness of the outbound programme. But the venue was still suspense for them.

All the students boarded the bus, the driver and lastly the professor also boarded. Though the students were shouting, laughing, joking and were in fun mood. Professor took their attendance. He divided all the students into two groups and made a leader in both the groups who will be responsible for the rest of the journey. Now they were ready to leave. Driver started the bus but the students were very curious to know, where were they going. Suddenly one of the student asked professor, "Sir, where are we going?"

"Well, we all are going to BSE" Professor replied.

"BSE???" All were surprised. This was indeed a big thing for the third semester students as it was related to their syllabus. It was like a dream destination for Sharon, she always wanted to work in one of those, NSE or BSE. BSE reminded Kapil about his first sight of Sharon. Vihaan also passed a smile to Kapil as he heard about the BSE. Kapil asked Sharon, "You have been to BSE, na?"

"How do you know?" She said.

"I know . . . ." Kapil gave her a mysterious smile, Sharon was still confused, "You are guessing, na?"

"Orange spaghetti, White shirt, Brown jeans, Cream peep toes . . . . still you feel I am guessing . . ." Kapil replied in a poetic way.

Sharon was awed by listening to him. It was really so strange for her. Throughout the journey then she kept on asking him . . . . but Kapil didn't reveal his dreams to her . . . .

"You mean Bombay stock exchange" asked one of the first semester student.

"Yes . . ." said Professor and laughed along with other students.

"OMG . . . . Vow we are going to see something, which we haven't yet . . . ." All the students were really excited to know about it, as they have till now only heard about it.

Professor sat on the first seat and all the students at the back. The journey of two and a half hours was spent with songs, fun, jokes, and lots of frolics. Professor knew that after all they all are children and once they are together, they will forget about the mishap and will reunite. At the Lonavala, they stopped for half an hour to have some food and snacks. They all forgot that few days back they had fought and today they were again enjoying together. Professor was successful in his endeavour of reuniting the two batches.

And after finishing its journey of two and a half hours, bus arrived near the dalaal street by 12:30 p.m. Since the road to the BSE was too narrow, hence they had to park the bus approx 10 meters away from the building of BSE. Soon they all started walking towards BSE. They can see the board of BSE on the top of the building from far away. The students saw many offices of insurance companies, broker's offices, who help the people to invest in stock market, on way to BSE, advocates office in front of the BSE which was accompanied by the three four security guards who were present there. On the edge of the building there was a big, wide screen which displayed the NDTV channel which read the details related to the status of various companies and their shares. Suddenly they saw two SUV, that reads Maharashtra police, came. A well uniformed person with good physique, of about 30-35 came out of the SUV, all the security guards and other officers present there saluted him, he was the Deputy Commissioner of Police. He, along with some of his officers went inside the building. There was a strong security check. Only people with the valid ID proofs were allowed to enter inside the gate. There were two check posts, one for men and another for women. Few students were roaming here and there and few were observing it. They were surprised to see that people who entered in the BSE office are not from any particular age. It seems to vary from early 20s to late 60s. Men, women, old ladies and gents all were going inside the building, this made them curious to know what's going inside. Though iiird sem students knew about its functioning but first sem students were more curious to know. They had the appointment of 1:30 p.m.-2:30 p.m. As per the schedule along with the professor, they all entered inside the building of Bombay Stock Exchange.

The Building had 6 lifts and a screen adjacent to each lift. One of the students pushed button on the screen and it suggested which lift to pick for that floor. Students went to one of the floor where they could see 100s of people working on the computer. The computer screens were full of numbers and name of company and the screen seemed rolling with red and blue colors. This reminded Kapil of Sharon's tab screen, which had the same look.

Each operator was also with telephone and was talking to someone. It looked as if there were systematic chaos all were talking, working on system but they knew what exactly was happening.

They then visited various other departments like Dept managing Corporates, Dept responsible for IPOs, Training Department, and Grievances Dept.

The Training Department had organised a session where they explained the history of BSE and how it works, the operations etc.

They were done with their visit inside the building by 3:20p.m. They took snaps and made videos as well they all came out of the building, filled with lots of energy, motivation and enthusiasm and satisfaction of being at BSE, They gained lots of knowledge on the investment in stock market.

Now, since all were hungry so they decided first to board the bus, respective leaders took the attendance of their team members, and then bus took them to the nearest restaurant. They had lunch together in a restaurant; students of both the semester were now talking and had again become friends.

The clock strike 5p.m. Though the students insisted to visit few of the places but professor asked the driver to move back to Pune, but in between he asked driver to get them through the SeaLink, the most beautiful bridge that connects Bandra to Worli, students took photos, they were mesmerized by the beauty of the architecture and sea all around, gave them a wonderful feeling. Then the bus reached CBD Belapur while crossing Andheri and other parts of Mumbai . . . . Now, the professor was relaxed. The clock struck 5:47pm. Professor was now sure that they will reach Pune by 7-8p.m. The bus reached Lonavala and had halted for half an hour. All the students had something to eat and they had snacks and came back to board the bus. And the bus again started moving towards Pune. It was 6:30p.m., due to cold weather it had started getting dark. Students were also now tired and most of them were taking nap, some listening to songs and some busy with their thoughts, some on facebook, some on chats etc. The bus was crossing a tunnel, suddenly the driver got a nap and he lost his control over the bus, as he regained his consciousness, he tried to stop the bus by putting brakes, but the bus was out of control and was sliding on the road and it got stuck to the small boundary of the road side. It was all deep valley surrounding the roads. The bus slipped off the road breaking the boundaries, all the students started screaming and everyone got frightened. The bus was about to fall but it was struck into a tree which was on the slope of the valley. They all stood still, girls started crying, boys were also frightened and threatened, to think about the consequences if they fall.

As the bus got stuck and became a bit stable, professor asked everyone to be on their place. He immediately made a call to the police to provide them help for their rescue and he called the Director to send another bus for them. He told them about their location and explained the situation.

Professor was also in the same status, as his students, but he knew his role, being a teacher he must not panic and had to act very carefully and sensibly. He first asked all the students to be at the back of the bus. They all were shouting and screaming aloud, professor asked all of them to keep quiet and listen to him carefully, by that time Sharon, Kapil, Vihaan, Nisaa, Chhabi and Ashok, all were finding the way to flee out of this situation. Soon Sharon found the door of the emergency exit at the second last window seat from the back. She, along with Kapil and Vihaan tried to open it, but suddenly bus jerked a little, professor asked them to do it slowly. They did it. Students got a hope, seniors made the order of preference in the following sequence: junior girls, junior boys, senior girls and then senior boys. As per their preference one by one they asked junior girls to go out from the window. As a single student jumps out of the window, the bus gets slide down a bit, this happened each time a student goes down. While students were busy in this professor thought he had to do something because he can see that bus was already swaying and in few minutes it will fall down. Professor immediately asked for the belts from all students, he joined them. He asked the students who were already rescued and on safer side to take help of some heavy vehicle passing by . . . . after few seconds they were able to stop a truck. He asked them to tie the one end of the belt rope to the truck tightly and one by one immediately all the students using the belt rope came out of the bus. As soon as all the students came out of the bus, the bus slided down more and its back tyre was only stucked in the tree and rest of the body was swaying only the driver who sat on the first seat of the bus was left. He was crying, praying to God to take care of his family, he lost all his hopes. But the professor decided that he had to save him anyhow. The length of the belt rope was short the bus driver's seat was a bit far from them. The professor went towards the tree. The tree was almost crumpled but its root were still intact and quite thick and strong. The roots of the tree were just near to the window of the bus. He slowly, with the help of belt rope, went downwards to hold the root. He sat in between the criss crossed roots, held them from one hand and offered his another hand to the driver. The driver had kept his eyes closed. Professor asked him to hold his hands. Driver was still in shock, as if he has accepted that he will die today. Professor again said, won't you like to give yourself one chance to save your life?. This time he listened to him and he too extended his hand to hold professor's hand. As he did, the bus again started sliding, professor said "Fast, come on you can do it"

"Driver stood on his seat, professor also slided a bit more towards the bus and again a jerking sound and driver galloped and held his hand tightly with both hands. As soon as he held his hands, bus made a loud jerk and fell down in the valley which was accompanied by a big sound of blast. But driver was still swinging in hands of Professor, Professor made a great effort and lifted him up and asked to hold the roots with one hand. And then

Professor pulled him up on the same root where he sat. And then with the help of the belt rope they both came up on the road. As soon as they reached up all the students shouted in happiness, they lifted the professor on their shoulders. All the juniors paid gratitude to their seniors, driver was on his knees, Professor was god for him, Shashank lifted him up and hugged him and said, "Dont worry we are safe now."

By that time, another bus from the college arrived and they all thanked God for their new lives and moved towards, Pune, with a new and unforgettable moment of their life.

Throughout the journey all were still in shock, that it could have been their last day on earth but indeed due to presence of mind, and with help of the professor, all were safe and sound.

"Vow!!! this is called a real hero." "Professor Shashank . . . zindabad, Professor Shashank zindabad . . ." Saloni started shouting. All the passengers, attendants and airhostesses looked at her. Mr. Ranade requested her to keep quiet.
"Really sir, what a man . . . . And sir, seems everything is set now . . . . Vihaan and Chhabi are progressing" she winked, "Soon Sharon and Kapil will also be couples . . ." "Great soon gonna be happy endings . . . Em i right . . . ?"

Saloni asked professor. Professor nodded in disagreement. Saloni added, "Then what?"

"There is a twist", Professor said

"O hh Is it . . ."
"Yes . . . . , Life is not so simple . . ."
"What?"
Professor again started . . . .

Mastering Mutual Funds

Continuous rains, it seemed the rain has become the part of curriculum. Everywhere there is water . . . Play ground was damped in water . . . it was so irritating that no one could even think of moving anywhere . . . or go for any outing or something.

All the students were getting bored. Ashok, Kapil, Vihaan, Nisaa and others were watching outside window to relax themselves. But Chhabi was fond of rains and rain drops, she was playing with the drops that fell on her face. She sat near the window intentionally, due to which water drops were coming on her as well. She just kept her face over to the window due to which water sprinkles on her face . . . which one by one as a drop slide down from her forehead to nose, then lips, then chins and then passing through neck they disappear . . . seemed as if they also tried to play with her then accompanied by second drop . . . Chhabi was enjoying all this, space after of when love is in the air everything seems to be beautiful . . . though she wasn't unaware that she was being captured by two eyes of Vihaan. Vihaan was continuously observing her. She was looking prettiest in her light pink color anarkali suit and chudidar with dark pink laced dupatta, her hair slightly tied with a clip at the back, which again rolled over her back, shoulders, face and keep touching her face. Her electrifying smile, her pious innocence, her cute face, her bright eyes and her beauty. He never found her so beautiful. He was just enjoying that moment. He thanked rains for this special moment. Perhaps both have similar feelings now. Gradually Kapil's impact on Chhabi was vanishing. Vihaan cannot resist himself to keep away from her. He went and sat near Chhabi. She smiled softly and blushed.

Kapil, who was then sick of rains and the environment, suddenly regained his lost enthusiasm when he saw, Sharon coming towards the lecture room. She was completely drenched. Kapil was stucked at the glance of Sharon. In that condition also she managed to look bold and hot. She was in her red multi colored spaghetti top, which has sticked to her body due to being wet and blue denim jeans, her hair was wet and curly, which she was trying to dry up through her fingers her favourite pink tabloid in hand with a hand bag hanged on one hand. As she entered the room, she sat on the seat and took out her shoes because they also were wet, took out a handkerchief from her bag and wiped her face and hand.

Kapil was just at the back of Sharon and in a very low voice he said, "Hi". She looked back and replied to him, "Hi" with a small smile. He just kept watching her, trickling down waters from her hair. Few of them rested on her soft shoulder and few slipped on through her hand to down. Watching this Kapil suddenly felt a desire to touch her. But he can't even dare to do that, he knew it. Her wet top which was stuck to her body, shows her perfect figure and she looked more attractive than ever. He thought, "Man!! why girls look so seducing when they are wet? . . .". Besides all that students had planned a surprise for their professor and all were keenly waiting for the professor. Till now everyone in the college came to know about the professor's bravery, management had decided to give him special award on Independence Day.

As soon as Prof. Shashank entered the class room, he was welcomed with a corporate clap as usual.

Immediately students came with a big giant greeting card, which they had purchased especially for their favourite professor. Kapil said, "Sir, whatever you have done for us is priceless, we cannot pay them back throughout our life, but yes this is our way to show you that how much we love you . . ." All the students clapped and Professor also got emotional and he thanked all the students for this beautiful gift. He said anything given by my students to me is precious for me."

Prof. Shashank's new get up of full sleeved shirts and waist coat gave him a more professional look and he looked more handsome than usual. Some students complimented him, some did hooting for his dashing look and thus he was welcomed by students. Professor just smiled.

"So, shall we proceed"
"Sure sir . . ."
"Well, today we will study about the investment in Share markets".

Immediately Kapil asked a question, "Sir i want to invest in Share market but I don't know how to Invest, i really don't have knowledge of that. Is there any way by which it can be done?" Vihaan, just next to him, was a silent observer, of course his silence was something which every girl was obsessed with.

"Kapil, you are always ready with the questions, this is something which makes me nervous before entering the classroom . . ." Professor said in humour.

":p ☺" Kapil's expression.

Professor sat on the chair and replied" Well, this is really a pertinent question most of the people don't invest in Stock market because they perceive it to be highly risky, moreover as you said they don't have knowledge and in real sense they don't want to risk their hard earned money."

"Also we have been taught from childhood that Stock Market is nothing but Sutta Bazar and no less than gambling". "Even many of our old movies have always depicted Stock Market in bad sense and every time the Hero or the character has lost his money whenever he invested in stock market."

Professor felt thirsty, he took a sip of water from the water filled glass kept on the podium, and started again, "But now the scenario has changed, with emergence of number of TV Channels on Stock Market, the psyche of common man is changing. Now very few people treat it as gambling but they still perceive the investment to be highly risky, thanks to various stock scams and their glorification by the media."

"But sir, i there any way by which we can get into market, reduce risk and gain what stock market gains are". Ashok asked . . .

"Yes absolutely", Professor replied, his eyes shone with excitement.
"Well, This can be achieved by . . . . a . . . a . . . a . . . i mean . . ." Professor went blank for a while, "a . . . could u please repeat the question"

Ashok replied, "Sir i asked that is there any way by which we can reduce risk and increase gains involved in stock markets?"

"Oh yes, Mutual Fund Way." "This is a solution which ensures that the risk is reduced considerably, knowledge of stock market is not necessary and while getting all these benefits you have privilege to earn the returns which stock market provides."

"Sir please tell us, I want to know the details of it, can u tell us how the MF works." Said Kapil.

"Yes why not. Let me explain you with simple example, Lets us go to the class and i will show you how MF works." He was tired but he decided to stand.

Again one of the students said "When we should invest, is there a right time or month. Can we invest when market goes down and sell when it's in peak. Is it possible?

Professor smiled and said "Yes October is one of the peculiarly dangerous months to speculate in stocks. The others are July, January, September, April, November, May, March, June, December, August and February.". Students started laughing but Professor calmed them down and then said. "It's really difficult to time the market, if it was possible, everyone would have made monies. Since it is difficult we go for Mutual fund and learn various techniques so that we take a sound and knowledgeable take on right investment and at right time".

Prof Shashank was a fantastic teacher who believed in demonstration and now he was going to demonstrate how Mutual Fund works.

The class was full. Students were eager to listen to the Professor.

Shashank started "How many of you want to buy bikes in six months or year or so?"

Students shouted "we all all" . . .

"Ok then why don't you buy?" . . . Shashank said, "we don't have Money, my all money is swallowed by my girl friend, my Dad is Kanjoos," there were variety of answers for the question raised.

Shashank again asked "How much you can spare from your expenses". The answers were between Rs.1000 to Rs.10000.

Now Prof Shashank was at his best, he asked "Are you ready to invest in stock market". The answer was big NO except for couple of students who said yes but their voice was calmed down by vociferous NO.

Prof. Shashank again shouted which brought him to cough, "Why Not?". "We don't know, Its risky, I don't like stock market, i have little money . . ." were the answers.

Prof Shashank took a sip of water and again roared "if I assure you that your Investment will be safe, You will get returns what stock market gives and you need not bother of how to invest, know how of stocks or anything related to market knowledge, now will you invest?".

Students shouted "Yes, we will but is it really possible?".

"Yes it is possible through MF method." Professor got excited while explaining further, "Now i will show you and prove you logically that whatever i have said is possible. We now have a corium of 50 students in our class. All have agreed to Invest in stock market. Now following will be the steps we will take to invest in the market

Pooling of Money: All 50 students as per their capacity will pool in fund which has to be invested in the stock market. Someone will invest Rs.1000 the other would Rs.4000 and it can be any amount as per your convenience.

Fund Manager: We need to find out someone who will be the person managing out Fund, Now he needs to be someone who has got excellent knowledge of the stock market. Since we do not have expert here, we shall ask Mahesh to help us as he is a stock consultant and is involved 24 hrs in research and analysis of companies.

Portfolio Designing: Now let us find out where all you want to invest. One student said he wants his pooled money to be invested in banking sector, other said in software and so there were almost all sectors companies where the students wanted to invest.

Fund Design: Since the Fund involves all different companies, we shall call the fund diversified.

Fund Management Charges: The Fund Manager who will invest the fund will not work free of cost and wud rather charge something. The charges would be on percentage on the pooled amount.

Investment of the Fund: The fund which is pooled is then invested as per the portfolio designed and the companies selected.

Returns: The Invested amount will fetch returns to be given in proportion of the invested amount of each individual.

He sat for a while to relax.

After a break of one minute, Shashank asked "Can anyone tell me how risk is reduced here". For a second there was pin drop silence in the class and then Chhabi answered breaking the silence "Since we are going to invest in various companies, the performance of all companies cannot go down at a time, therefore it reduces the risk and gives you decent returns". Vihaan was impressed by her intelligence.

"Fantastic, marvellous," Shashank said excitedly.

Nisaa asked "if there are other students who want to get on the bandwagon and also want to get returns, can we allow them afterwards?"

Yes and No was the answer from Prof Shashank.

"You need to understand the Concept of Open Ended and Closed ended fund to answer the question raised by Nisaa". Shashank said in excited voice. He was enjoying as lot of questions were raised and he knew the more the questions the more interesting the class would get.

Shashank shared the slide:

Open Ended Fund: In these schemes the mutual fund continuously offers to sell and repurchase its unit at net asset value (NAV). Investor here can enter and exit the scheme any time during the life of fund. Open ended schemes do not have a fixed corpus. The corpus of the fund increases or decreases depending on the purchase and redemption of units by investors.

Closed Ended Fund: It has a fixed corpus and a stipulated maturity period ranging between 2-5 years. Investor can invest in the schemes when it is launched. The schemes remain open not more than 45 days during launch. Investors can buy units only from the market, once initial subscription is over, they are listed on exchanges where they can be baught and sold.

We now examine the different kinds of funds on the basis of their investments. The approaches to equity investing could be diversified or undiversified, growth, income, sector rotators, value, or market-timing based.

Each mutual fund scheme has a particular investment policy and the fund manager has to ensure that the investment policy is not breached. The policy is laid right at the outset when the fund is launched and is specified in the prospectus, the 'Offer Document' of the scheme.

The investment policy determines the instruments in which the money from a specific scheme will be primarily invested. Based on these securities, mutual funds can be broadly classified into

Equity funds (growth funds and income funds), Bond funds, Money market funds, Indexfunds, etc.

Shashank shared another slide:

Equity Funds are considered to be the more riskier funds as compared to other fund types but they also provide higher returns than other funds. Its is advisable that the investor looking at equity funds should be invested for longer period ie for term more than 3 years.

Money Market/Liquid Funds invest in short term (maturing within 1 year) interest bearing debt instruments. These securities re highly liquid and provide safety of the investments.

Hybrid Funds are those whose portfolio includes blend of equity, debt and money market securities. They have equal proportion of debt and equity.

Debt Funds invest in medium to long term debt instruments issued by private companies, banks, financial institutions or Government.

Gilt Funds are nothing but government securities in India. They have medium to long term maturity period, issued by Government of India has no credit risk and provide safelt of principal to the investors.

Exchange Traded Funds (ETF) provide investors with dual benefit of closed end fund and open end mutual fund. They follow stock market indices and are traded on exchanges as single stock at index prices.

Fund of Funds do not invest in financial or hysical assets but do it in other mutual fund schemes offered by different Asset Management Companies (AMC).

Thus finished the Professor, but he found students blank. Confusion was clearly visible on their faces but then Professor said that he will discuss about the things in detail later with practical application the concept will be easier to understand and grasp. Ok, that's all for today. Thank you and professor left. The bell also rang to show the timings.

As Professor left the class, students also left the classroom. Most of the students went to the canteen, some went for the next lecture, some in library and some were in the garden. The mishap had strengthened the bonding amongst seniors and juniors and Sharon, Chhabi, Vihaan, Kapil, Ashok and Nisaa, they all have become good friends and spent most of their times together.

Invest in Bonds

The students gathered in the classroom, they were discussing about the investment decisions. As they were well aware that professor can ask them any question any time, if fail to respond, he humiliates in such a way that the person remembers it throughout his life. So, they have started the practice of revising whatever he taught in the classroom. Sharon was a step ahead, she was going through a text book on SAPM which talks about investments in bonds . . . simultaneously she was busy on her tab as well.

Kapil, who was usually accompanied by Vihaan, was today alone busy on one of the book on SAPM but his main attention was towards . . . . well you know whom ;) and Vihaan was busy with Chhabi and her talks . . .

And then enters the Professor Shashank along with the ringing of bell. Students welcome him with their usual way. Professor starts with a statement that besides mutual funds one must also make investment in bonds. He adds, "Stock market is always exciting cause its scrutinised by experts, covered by newspapers and stories of people getting rich and gaining wealth are common in Stock Market. Bonds on the other hand don't have the similar sex appeal and is very sterile and boring especially when the bulls are on the move. However when the market crashes and bulls take over the significance and virtues of the Bonds are reminded. I would always suggest everyone needs to have some portion of the portfolio invested in bonds."

Though the confusion still prevailed . . . and Nisaa asks in confusion, "But, sir what is bond?" Other students said in unison. Professor said," Oh! Hadn't i told you about bonds?" He was confused for a second.

But then he smiled and said, "Ok . . . luk . . . Just as people need money, so do companies and governments. A company needs funds to expand into new markets, while governments need money for everything from infrastructure to social programs. The problem large organizations run into is that they typically need far more money than the average bank can provide. The solution is to raise money by issuing bonds (or other debt instruments) to a public market. Thousands of investors then each lend a portion of the capital needed." Taking a sip of water from the glass, he said "Really, a bond is nothing more than a loan for which you are the lender. The organization that sells a bond is known as the issuer. You can think of a bond as an IOU given by a borrower (the issuer) to a lender (the investor)."

But there was still confusion in students mind, they started murmuring, finally Ashol asked, "But sir, what would the investor get?

"Good Question" Professor was now more excited because he expected this question and replied, "Of course, nobody would loan his or her hard-earned money for nothing. The issuer of a bond must pay the investor something extra for the privilege of using his or her money. This "extra" comes in the form of interest payments, which are made at a predetermined rate and schedule. The interest rate is often referred to as the coupon. The date on which the issuer has to repay the amount borrowed (known as face value) is called the maturity date. Bonds are known as fixed-income securities because you know the exact amount of cash you'll get back if you hold the security until maturity."

"For example, say you buy a bond with a face value of Rs1,000, a coupon of 8%, and a maturity of 10 years. This means you'll receive a total of Rs.80 (Rs1,000*8%) of interest per year for the next 10 years. Actually, because most bonds pay interest semi-annually, you'll receive two payments of Rs.40 a year for 10 years. When the bond matures after a decade, you'll get your Rs 1,000 back."

Well now students were able to get him, but the insecurity that prevails along with bonds and stocks now was another question in their mind. And soon Vihaan asked, "Sir, I have heard that bond does not give as much return as Stock then why bother with Bonds?"

Professor laughed and replied, "HIGH RISK will give you CHANCE to earn HIGH RETURNS, however does it mean you start putting everything into Lottery Tickets expecting high returns. No in the similar fashion you do not invest everything into stock. Bonds are appropriate any time you cannot tolerate the short-term volatility of the stock market. Take two situations where this may be true:

Retirement—The easiest example to think of is an individual living off a fixed income. A retiree simply cannot afford to lose his/her principal as income for it is required to pay the bills.

Shorter time horizons—Say a young executive is planning to go back for an MBA in three years. It's true that the stock market provides the opportunity for higher growth, which is why his/her retirement fund is mostly in stocks, but the executive cannot afford to take the chance of losing the money going towards his/her education. Because money is needed for a specific purpose in the relatively near future, fixed-income securities are likely the best investment.

Now, students were able to understand the concept of Bonds. Professor was in form . . . and then another question was shot up by Kapil, "What are the characteristics of Bond?"

"Interesting", Professor replied, "Bonds have a number of characteristics of which you need to be aware. All of these factors play a role in determining the value of a bond and the extent to which it fits in your portfolio."

He shared his slide:

Par Value: Principal amount paid to investors upon maturity of the bond, and is also known as the face value. Coupon: Interest rate paid on the par value of the bond to the investor.

Maturity: It is the term of the bond. E.g. the date on which the issuer repays the principal amount of the bond

Put option: It gives right to the investor to redeem the bond at a fixed price within a specified time. Put is when the customer comes and forecloses the transaction

Call Option: It gives right to the issuer to buy back the bond at a fixed price within a specified time. Call is when the company calls the client to foreclose

Current yield :It is calculated as annual coupon rate divided by current market price

Yield to Maturity (YTM) :YTM is the internal rate of return, an investor would realize if "Bought the bond at a particular price" and "Received the entire coupon payments" and "Reinvested the coupons at this same YTM rate" and "Received the principal at maturity". YTM is used for comparing bonds, with different coupons, maturities and prices and is quoted for trading purposes.

Yield curve: A curve that shows the relationship between yields and maturity dates for a set of similar bonds at a given point in time can be termed as Yield Curve. If we plot maturity periods of the bonds on the X-axis and the coupon rates of the bonds on the Y-axis we get a curve known as the Yield Curve is also known as Term Structure of Interest Rates.

Yield Spread: It is the difference in or additional Yield required of a particular bond as compared to the yield of a benchmark security—(Govt. Security) to account for the risk of default by the borrower.

Credit Rating: Credit risk assessments are carried by external credit rating agencies. E.g.: CRISIL (Credit Rating & Information Services of India Ltd.), ICRA (Investment Credit Rating Agency), CARE (Credit Analysis & Research) Etc. Agencies Rate the specific issues of debt instrument of non-government borrowers.

Kapil was so curious about bonds that he kept on asking questions again and again and his next question was. "Sir Can you give example of some of the ratings agencies which rates Bonds". Professor replied, "Yes, why not."

"The major rating agencies in the U.S.: Moody's, Standard and Poor's and Fitch Ratings, where as in Inida it is CRESIL, ICRA and CARE.

Professor was now more happy because the session was directed towards a very interesting part and he said, "Well, now am going to tell you a very interesting thing about Bonds". "What sir? What sir?" Students were also curious to know about it.

"Do you know that price of bonds fluctuate and change on daily basis."

"Really??" "But how it is possible, sir?" were their questions.

"Yes . . . ." Professor said, "A bond's price changes on a daily basis, just like that of any other publicly-traded security. Up to this point, we've talked about bonds as if every investor holds them to maturity. It's true that if you do this you're guaranteed to get your principal back; however, a bond does not have to be held to maturity. At any time, a bond can be sold in the open market, where the price can fluctuate—sometimes dramatically."

Chhabi then suddenly asked, "Sir, shall be the yield on maturity?"

"Well dear, these matters are always more complicated in real life. When bond investors refer to yield, they are usually referring to Yield To Maturity (YTM). YTM is a more advanced yield calculation that shows the total return you will receive if you hold the bond to maturity."

"The relationship of yield to price can be summarized as follows: when price goes up, yield goes down and vice versa. Technically, you'd say the bond's price and its yield are inversely related."

"Here's a commonly asked question: How can high yields and high prices both be good when they can't happen at the same time? The answer depends on your point of view. If you are a bond buyer, you want high yields. A buyer wants to pay Rs800 for the Rs1,000 bond, which gives the bond a high yield of 12.5%."

After a long time going through details Sharon asked Professor, "Sir what about its price in the market?" "Well, must say a good question, As far as the prices in the market are concerned, when interest rates fall, the prices of bonds in the market rise, thereby lowering the yield of the older bonds and bringing them into line with newer bonds being issued with lower coupons."

Sharon immediately did something on her tab, she and her tab had become a puzzle for Kapil. But this is something she never shared to anyone. Nisaa who was busy in jotting down the points suddenly made a query, "Sir, does the bonds have types?"

"Yupz, of course." "Many like:" and he shared the slide to the students.

Government Bonds

In general, fixed-income securities are classified according to the length of time before maturity. These are the three main categories:

Bills

debt securities maturing in less than one year.

Notes

Debt securities maturing in one to 10 years.

Bonds

Debt securities maturing in more than 10 years.

Corporate Bonds a short term bonds issued by corporate.

Zero-Coupon Bonds appreciate gradually and earnings accumulate until maturity, when the bond is redeemable at full face value.

"So, does it means bonds are something which we buy, right." Said Kapil.

"Yes of course" Professor said while sitting on the chair and took a sip of water.

"But how do we buy bond?"

"Oh! you can purchase Bonds from me . . . . i mean through brokers or online brokers like ICICI Direct, HDFC securities, Angel Broking, Sharekhan etc." said Sharon ":p"

"Well said, Sharon. By the way that's all for today . . . thank you . . . bbyee"

"Thank you sir . . ." Students in unison. Bell rang and the lecture ended.

As the professor left, students also started leaving the classroom. Sharon also left the class for canteen. Kapil followed her to the canteen and as she was about to stretch the chair, he galloped and did it for her. She was surprised to see him and hesitatingly she sat and asked, "Yes . . . wanna say something." Kapil sat and he first ordered two cold coffees for Sharon and himself. Then he settled and looked at Sharon, and he found her face with a big question mark. Sharon again said, "What?" Kapil said, "nothing, just wanted to talk to u."

"About what?"

"About your tab."

"What?" replied Sharon trying to hide her tab.

"What do you do all the time on your tab? I mean i see you always busy on your tab."

"Well, i don't do anything . . . . that is something personal and i cannot tell you"

"But it resembles to the one I saw in the BSE."

Sharon was taken aback. She stood to leave, but then Kapil asked her to sit to have the coffee at least.

They both had coffee together, they talked about the lectures and then Sharon left the canteen for some important task.

Fundamental Analysis: Made Easy

Another Saturday came with a new concept. Students were already seated in their usual places; the new thing today was that Nisaa sat beside Sharon. They were discussing about the lecture.

Nisaa: "Well must say, you have gud command over the subject."

Sharon: "Oh!! No, its jxt dat, i have interest, which makes me to learn more abt it. Thats it . . . btw thanks" "I love to know about market trends, . . . this is what fascinates me . . ."

Nisaa: "Great, em impressed, u r more knowledgeable than ur age . . ."

Sharon with a freak smile said: "We have to go long way . . . . right . . . . \m/"

Nisaa: "Yuppz . . . \m/

Then they started discussion about the subject. Nisaa told Sharon that sometimes she finds mutual funds and stocks boring and sometimes interesting. Whereas Stocks and mutual funds always fascinates Sharon and she rarely get bored of it. She was quite excited that today they will be taught about the fundamental analysis of stocks.

Professor entered the Class. Today he was in black cartridge blazer and matching attire. He looked most handsome ever and as he entered the class he was complimented by many students. The class was full packed waiting to know what Prof would take. Professor tried hard to speak louder and said "Today we are going to have recap of whatever we have learnt so far." And so the recap session started, Professor started asking questions and to his surprise almost 90% of topics he had discussed, the students were able to recollect and explain him in detail. Professor was impressed, the class was really above average and he wanted to further challenge their intellect.

But suddenly Ashok got up from his chair "Sir I think we should always invest in good company, they are the safest bet".

Professor replied "Investors must keep in mind that there's a difference between a good company and a good stock. After all, you can buy a good car but pay too much for it. We are here to make money, not to show our loyalty to any company,. So we are bothered for good stock which will give us decent returns".

Professor now raised a question "How would you analyse a stock". Students knew Professor even though was not a miser but he will never spend a single pie unless he sees value for money in that deal. He again rephrased his question "The money we have is hard earned money. We cannot invest in any stock until we get all evidences and indicators suggesting of the same. So how you check that a particular stock is the right stock for investment?". The question was loud and clear. Few said we shall take tips given by Brokers, some were of opinion that TV channels particularly CNBC gives right investment tips on stocks.

Professor said "There are primarily 3 different types of investors who post on the message boards.

1. Those who don't know anything: approx. 10%
2. Those who know a little: approx. 10%
3. Those who don't realize they don't know anything: approx. 80%

And i don't want any of my students to be part any of these three groups, I want perfect answer. This will be an assignment cum project. Now I want volunteers who would do this." Nobody rose from the seat cause today was the last day and field work break would start from the next day.

As usual Sharon stood up, she would never let down Professor's word. Kapil, Vihaan and Ashok followed Sharon as they couldn't afford to leave her standing all alone, Chabbi followed Vihaan . . . and the trail continued till there were volunteers.

Professor said "Fine I am not going to take class today, you six volunteers have taken responsibility to answer my question. The field work break is for 6 days and so we shall meet again after this. Also I expect the volunteers would give us in depth knowledge on the techniques to analyse the stock."

The class was over, students ran as this was the last class of the day and they knew once they will leave for field work they won't be able to do anything and so, Sharon, Kapil, Vihaan, Ashok, Chabbi and others were standing, thinking what to do. They were not able to formulate any strategy to counter this challenge. Sharon said "Don't worry, let us go to Library and see if we can get anything on analysis of the stocks". The idea was good they all were in the Library and all books on stocks available in library were on the table, each one was scanning, running through the contents. Finally after an hr of deliberations, they concluded that there are basically two ways by which the stock can be analysed

Fundamental Analysis of Stock
Technical Analysis of stock.

The time 6 days for field work and this was the challenge to complete the task before that and had to prepare presentation. They also knew Prof Shashank is a hard nut and he will really put them in soup if they don't prepare the subject properly.

The team was divided Ashok, Vihaan, Nisaa were in the team who would prepare for Fundamental analysis while Sharon, Kapil, Chabbi were in the team Technical Analysis.

Sharon from one book started reading out loudly.

The methods used to analyze securities and make investment decisions fall into two very broad categories: fundamental analysis and technical analysis.

Fundamental analysis involves analyzing the characteristics of a company in order to estimate its value. Technical analysis takes a completely different approach; it doesn't care one bit about the "value" of a company or a commodity.

Technicians (sometimes called chartists) are only interested in the price movements in the market.

The initial part looked interesting so the team Technical Analysis borrowed books on Technical Analysis and decided to meet next day evening at Café California to plan put next move.

Making of a Presentation

All three Sharon, Kapil and Chabbi gathered at a Café. It was evident from their faces that something was not right. Sharon said "What's up buddy?, how was the day and . . ." before she could say more Kapil bumped in "Bullshit this is all Charts and I am not able to understand how to even hold it and what and where to see. Man I am lost".

Chabbi followed "Same case with me sometimes they talk about volume, breakout, resistance, pattern, it was all Latin and Hebrew for me".

Sharon said "You are right this is not easy and if we try ourselves it will take time and time is our problem. We can't afford to waste time, so some other plan has to be chalked out".

They all were in deep thought, suddenly Kapil shouted, "I have an idea. In today's paper there is an ad on Technical Analysis seminar cum training program. It is of two days and they claim, it will enable us to take proper decision using tools of Technical analysis. If you want I will call them and take further details".

Sharon said, "Go ahead, obviously it will cost us fortune as the Pocket Money which we get is meager but we don't have any other choice. Either we attend workshop or go empty handed and head down in front of Prof Shashank". Nobody was ready for second option so they all decided to get workshop fee by hook or crook at any cost, beg borrow or steal was their temporary motto.

Kapil collected the information, the workshop was conducted by renowned TA expert with experience of more than 18 years. He has seen the ups and downs of the market, had predicted the market crash of 2008 and had also seen affect of scams. Further he was famous for minimizing theory and maximizing the real applicability of the Technical Analysis tools. The Fee for Two day session was Rs.5000 per person. They could have assigned one person to attend the workshop but no one was confident whether he or she can understand wholly in the workshop and of course 3 brains are better than 1.

They had dinner together, and they all left for home.

The 2nd team was on the task of exploring stock analysis method called Fundamental Analysis. They referred various books, discussed with number of Brokers and finally they were ready with the presentation. They were quite happy as they had done their job.

Scary Night

Since it was quite late approx 10:30p.m. Chhabi came on her scooty itself, so she managed to go . . . But Sharon's house was a little far but she went out to try for auto rickshaw. Kapil had his four wheeler, though he wanted to give her a lift, but he knew if he will ask her she will refuse, so he just waited to let her ask herself for lift, that will be more polite in Sharon's case. And he was right, when Sharon couldn't find any rickshaw, she reluctantly had to ask for lift from Kapil, though she didn't wanted to take, but circumstances made her to do so.

Both of them were in Kapil's sedan. Sharon's house was exactly at a distance of one and a half hours. The car ran on the dreary and lonely road. There was no voice audible except the breath of two so called friends . . . That silence was killing Kapil, he wanted to talk to Sharon but Sharon didn't take any initiative for talks. Kapil saw her face, which was very quiet and expressionless. On the other hand Sharon was feeling uncomfortable being with Kapil because she knew that he has intentions for her, she was fighting in her conscious mind: one said why you took lift from Kapil when u know dat he likes you . . . Other mind said that was the only option I had . . . . and in this way she was trying to justify herself, why did she took lift and similar thoughts were going in her mind. It was becoming irresistible for Kapil to keep quiet and that too in front of Sharon, with whom he always wanted to talk. Millions of thoughts were crossing Kapil's mind. How to start, where to start, what to say and thus a virtual brainstorming session started in his mind. After lot of churning of thoughts, he started the conversation, "So, hwzz ur studies going on?"

"Hmm . . . fine" Sharon replied concisely.

"k . . ."

"Well, must say u hv good knowledge, on the subject . . . and that too being junior also . . ."

"Thanks . . ."

Car slowed down . . . gharr . . . gharrr . . . ghaarrrr. "Ohh . . . shitt!!!" Kapil said in worry.

"What happened?"

"a . . . a . . . No, nothing" finally car stopped.

"I em sorry, dear . . . but i think that there is something wrong with the car and it's not starting . . . ." making efforts to start the car but there was nothing more than gharr . . . gharrrr . . . gharrr . . . . sound.

Kapil went outside to check the engine if there was something wrong in the engine but couldn't find anything . . . . and came back in the car . . . . Sharon was annoyed and cursed herself, "Oh shitt man! why i took lift from him . . ." Kapil made a call to his home to send someone for help. Kapil requested Sharon not to panic and promised her that he will drop her home asap. It was about 10:45pm, and they were on the lonely road waiting for help . . . Since it was cold Kapil had closed all the windows . . . Only the headlights were on and they were trying to relax . . .

Suddenly they heard a noise of someone knocking on the window glass. Kapil pressed the button to open the window pane . . . and a strange man with a masculine build, approx 5'11" heighted with a big moustache in dark clothes and jacket . . . . asked them, "What's goin on?"

Kapil asked, "Who are you?"

Man replied in a rude voice, "Crime branch"

Kapil was shocked to hear and immediately went out of the car, Sharon also followed him. Man again asked," Whats going on, here?" This time his voice was more rude.

Sharon said, "Sir, We are waiting for the help, actually our car has broke down." Kapil nodded in agreement.

"Don't try to fool me, I know very well, what was going on?"

"What do u mean, v r students not a terrorist or a prostitute . . . hw can u say like this . . . . Uuu . . . !" Kapil tried to make her silent.

"Ohh look at her courage, must say lady that u r quite smart, but ur smartness will not work in front of me . . . got it photo khichwa k paper mein chhapwa dunga jhootha ilzaam laga k samaj gaye na . . . ."

Kapil understood that how to tackle him. He went to the man and politely said, "Sir please forgive us, we will not repeat this mistake, whatever u want just tell me" and he took out his purse from his pocket. Man's eyes brightened with the glance of notes and Kapil gave him whatever he had in his purse and man was satisfied and about to leave.

Suddenly Sharon came again and asked," Hey, show me your i-card. What is the proof that you are from crime branch? I will go to police and make a complaint against you. You are trying to suck the common people and think we can't do anything. She took out her phone and dialled 100.

Man got annoyed and said, "Abhi ek laafa padega kaan ke neeche, dimmag thikane aa jayega . . . Abhi jhootha charge laga ke under kar dunga samjhi na . . . yes am not crime bramch officer am a police officer aur jyada hekdi dikhayi to jail mein band kar dunga . . . . hme sudharne chale hainnn . . . khud raat raat bhar lladkon ke saath aiyyashi krte hain aur phir police ke peeche padte hain ki hmare saath ye ho gaya . . . wo ho gaya . . . ."

Murmuring man left the place.

Sharon was burning in anger. She turned towards Kapil and asked him, "Why did u gave him bribe? When we are not guilty, then what was the need to give him bribe . . . ?

Sharon has the point but Kapil said politely, "He was here for the money itself, that was the only way to get rid off him."

Sharon couldn't understand this . . . and in few minutes Kapil's uncle came with another car and he dropped Sharon at her home and then went to Kapil's home. Kapil was extremely sorry for the incident, he never wanted this to happen and that too when Sharon was with him. He wanted her to cool down and to make her normal. He just called Nisaa and asked her to talk to Sharon. He thought perhaps Sharon might feel better after talking to Nisaa. It was weird, shameful and embarrassing moment for Sharon. No one has ever talked to her like this, though she was used to the darkest of the incidents in her life but this was something humiliating and she could not bear this. As soon as he laid down on his cosy bed, he found a notification, it was a note added by Sharon on Facebook:

Days which were boom of heaven,
Filled with frolics when accompanied by maven . . . .

Are now eclipsed by the dawn of emptiness,
And life has become a part of filthiness . . . .

Each day my soul struggles to cope,
Which was someday filled with hope . . . .

I never felt it when u wr wid me before, now it is more accurate when u aren't anymore . . . .
Walking on a dark path fill of silent snags, i miss you n wish u come and save me from slags . . . .

The notification itself shows him, about her feeling, but he wasn't able to understand for whom she had dedicated this poem.

A New Beginning!

Next day Kapil called Sharon at Cafe Coffee Day near to his house. Sharon and Kapil have now become friends to some extent, so she came to meet him at CCD. She was looking cool and soothing in her sky blue frock, which was till her knee. Her brown hair was the most beautiful thing that give her more beauty and grace. She came towards Kapil slowly walking towards him, he was continuously staring at her, he can't put his eyes off from her. This feeling was new to him, he was confused of his feelings. He never felt similar for any girl. Soon Sharon smiled was in front of him, immediately Kapil got up stretched a chair for her to offer a seat. And Sharon smiled in response to his politeness and sat on the chair. She asked him for reason to call her. Kapil suggested to order something before starting the conversation. Sharon ordered one cold coffee and a veg roll and Kapil ordered one expresso and a chicken momo. Then Kapil started, "Am sorry for 'that day', you know my intention was not to hurt you. In fact I can't even imagine the same."

Soon their order was served.

"Its okk . . . I understand" said Sharon sipping the cold coffee. Kapil can see the neutrality in her eyes. He again tried to gain her interest. He continued the conversation which lasts till the coffee does.

"So, r u ok now? . . ."

"hmmm . . ."

"So, wats your opinion about the lectures"

"yup . . . they r damn gud, prof. Shashank is indeed a great faculty."

Again a pause . . . . for a minute . . . .

He kept on observing her face. Today no one was there to disturb him from observing her face. Sharon too had mixed feelings, though she was aware about the feelings of Kapil, but she can't stop him from continuously watching her. She was feeling a bit shy and kept on looking to her coffee mug, because she doesn't have the courage to face Kapil. After both of them were done, Kapil said, "You look so innocent like a baby. You know wat . . . ." and suddenly he stopped.

"What?" said Sharon,

"Nothing"

"temme na . . ."

"I can see God in you"

Sharon was moved by his statement. She said, "But I don't even pray."

"But, I can see Him in your innocence, simplicity, truthfulness and piousness."

Sharon was unable to say anything, this was the first time someone has made such a comment on her. Also if he was flattering her, she liked his style. Though in reply she could only smile.

Sharon thanked Kapil for the coffee and was just about to leave, he said, "I wanna say something." Sharon said, "What?"

He said hesitatingly, "I will never ever hurt you and you can ask for any help, anytime, am always with you . . ."

"thnks"

Sharon was stunned by his words, she looked into his eyes . . . she was trying to read his eyes . . . . she tried to read his feelings . . . . she was a bit happy that there is someone who understands her well . . . . she was a bit scared that if he knew everything about her . . . . she was afraid that what he will think if he will come to know about her . . . . she was afraid that now everyone would know the real Sharon . . . . she doesn't want anyone to know about her darker side . . . . In confusion Sharon left the place without uttering a word.

Kapil also tried to read her eyes . . . . but he found that suddenly those eyes were seemed like an ocean which has lots of waves and shores inside, the usual bright light was missing . . . there was a fear in those eyes . . . . there was a pain in those eyes . . . . there was a grief in those eyes . . . . there was something very weird in those eyes . . . . but he thought that wasn't right time to stop Sharon.

Kapil texted her to let him know when she reaches home. Kapil reached his home after half an hour. Soon a beep sound and,

"Hey! I have reached my place . . . , thanks" message from Sharon.

Kapil replied, "take care". As Kapil went to his room to take rest or to rewind the moment when he was with Sharon, about half an hour later, again a beep sound, there was a notification on facebook . . . . it was by Sharon, she added something to her 'Notes' in facebook, in no time he clicked on the link, it was a poem:

Loved u as a loosen soul,
Keeping my breath in control,
I was in a lost battle of life.
U brought me some hope and light,
Glad and joy suddenly came to me,
Was unknown to the darker side of we,
Dreams crashed as the destiny showed its truth,

I was left with nothing and no worth.
Lost my everything to death,
Wonder how i am still here with my breath,
U . . . U . . . why u left me with life so cruel,
Mine Love to u was true and mutual,
Punish me for my misdeeds,
Come and annoy on my stupidness,
Hate me for my mistakes . . .
But please come back . . .
I am waiting for U . . .
With my heart filled of love for U . . . .

Kapil was astonished to see such notification, what does it mean? Is it only a poem or her original feeling? Is there someone in her life? Few minutes back Kapil was so happy about the thought of being with Sharon and now he felt as if he has fallen from great height. He wasn't able to digest it. But, he decided that he will find out the truth behind the Sharon's poem.

Analysis by 'Future Experts'

Field work break was over, students were back in college . . . Campus, where silence prevailed, again became lively by the chits and chats of the students. They seemed happy to meet their friends . . . they were glad to reunite.

But the students of SAPM course were in a different mood. They were happy, nervous and sad were in mixed emotions. They were worried for they were supposed to give presentation in front of professor. And this gonna be not an easy one . . . So all the students with their team members moved to the classroom. Some were busy on their notebooks, some busy with their notes, some on book, some revising, some discussing the demo questions which they may be asked and in this way all were busy with their presentations.

The Class was full. The students were talking to each other in soft voices. They were apprehensive and were not sure whether the two teams would deliver the goods as promised.

Soon the bell rang and with a delay of one minute Professor entered the class. Students stood with the corporate clap.

He passed a smile and started asking students about Diwali and its celebrations. All students were also happy to see his professor. They replied in unison "Fabulous, mast, awesome, fantastic etc . . ." Professor added, "If I am not wrong, I had given some task . . . mmm what was it", Then all the students started talking at a time . . . It was on how to analyse Stock . . . was the answer.

"Yes and where are the guys, have they disappeared?", Professor tried to chuckle. "No Sir was the reply", and there stood Sharon in her light blue jeans and black t-shirt, confident as usual. "We are ready for the presentation. Ashok is ready with Fundamental Analysis and me and my team will present Technical Analysis.

They knew that professor will take them to task if they fail to do justice with the presentation.

Ashok took the stage and started explaining. He said "The market is like a beautiful woman—endlessly fascinating, endlessly complex, always changing, always mystifying". There was loud clap on the startling statement by Ashok.

Ashok said "Now time has come to unravel and demystify the beautiful woman. I am going to explain you, how you can understand the market and make informed investment decision. Great investment opportunities come around when excellent companies are surrounded by unusual circumstances that cause the stock to be misappraisal We have to make use of this unfortunate circumstances, analyse the stock and do the cherry picking".

"There are basically two ways by which a stock or company can be analysed or ratified to be fit for investment.

Fundamental Analysis

Technical Analysis.

Now let me explain you what Fundamental Analysis means", Ashok was in full mood, he was thinking as if he has been teaching and taking training programs for years.

"Fundamental Analysis is based on the fact that every share has certain Intrinsic value at a period of time, which changes due to certain internal and external factors. The theory propounds that one should purchase share when it is available below intrinsic value and sell when it is above." Ashok said

One student had a question mark on his face, he asked "What is intrinsic value and how do we find it (?)".

Ashok replied "Intrinsic . . . .—"

But calculation of Intrinsic Value comes last in the Analysis. There are many Internal and external factors which affects the value. Now I am going to explain you step by step process in Fundamental Analysis . . .

Step 1

Geo Politico—Economic Analysis

International Events impact industries and companies like wars, recession etc.

Possibility of devaluations of one's currency for example the devaluation of Rs in India affected stock market adversely.

Foreign debts can be an enormous burden which would eat into a company's results.

Inflation erodes purchasing power. Low inflation indicates stability and companies prosper at such time.

Domestic savings accelerated economic growth

Good GDP has a good impact on the market.

Budgetary deficit resulting from excess governmental spending stimulate the economy.

Business Economic cycle has a direct impact on industry and individual companies.

IIP numbers, Employability data affects market.

Four stages of economic cycle, depression, recovery, boom and recession affects market accordingly and keeping it in mind the investment decision has to be taken.

Step 2

Industry or Sector Analysis

It is better to invest in evergreen industries. Results of cyclical industries are volatile.

It is safer to invest in Industries not subject to Govt controls.

Investor should consider competition, as greater the completion lesser the profit.

It is important to determine cycle. They are entrepreneurial or sunrise, expansion or growth, stabilization or maturity and decline or sunset.

Investor should purchase in the first two stages and disinvest at the maturity.

Step 3

Company or Specific Stock Analysis

It is the Final Stage of Fundamental Analysis

Areas to be examined are the company, the results and ratio and cash flow.

Management

Management is the single most important factor on which the future of the company rests.

In India two types of management are there Family and Professional.

The investor should check integrity of managers.

Annual report

The Investors should read between and beyond the lines of an annual report to determine the state of the com

Ratios

Ratios are the most important entities which tell you the story of the company.

The ratios are broken into 4 broad categories

Profit and Loss Ratios

Balance Sheet Ratio

Financial Statement to Market ratios

Various other ratios in combination are used to find out the strength of the company

Market Value ratio

Earnings per Share ratio

PEG

P/E

Liquidity Ratio

Leverage Ratio

Book Value

Cash Flow

Cash Flow statement will enable the investor to determine how is the company's cash earnings and how the company is being financed

The statement begins with the cash in hand at the beginning of the period and then details the source and amounts of funds received and the manner they were applied ending with the final cash in hand.

It strips the accounting statements of the creative accounting

Manoj said "What you have explained is ok but is there any way by which we can decide which parameters are important when we analyse a particular stock?. Is there any way by which we can give weightage to each factor in FA?".

"You are absolutely right. Now I am going to display excel sheet which has all the factors and importance to be given to it. I have given weightagie to each factor and if the stock gets more than 60 points we say the stock is Fundamentally strong and is a good investment bet.

Fundamental Analysis

Name Of the Company :

Sector:

Date :

Items	Economic Analysis	Type	Score	Scale— Rating
		Wt=22		Maximum
1	Govt Policy towards Industry	Desc		4
2	GDP	Nos		4
3	Inflation	Nos		4
4	Interest rates applicable	Desc		3
5	BOP—Foreign Reserves	Nos		3
6	Tax Structure	Desc		4
	Industry Analysis	**Wt=15**		
1	Type of Industry	Desc		4
2	Industry Life Cycle	Desc		2
3	Labour Issues If any	Desc		3
4	Cost Structure and Profitability	Desc		4
5	Nature of Product	Desc		2

	Company Analysis	Wt=63		
1	Competition	Desc		5
2	Management Style	Desc		5
3	Growth in last 5 years	Nos		5
4	Operating Efficiency/Margins	Nos		5
5	Capital Structure	Nos		5
6	EPS	Nos		5
7	PE Ratio	Nos		5
8	PEG	Nos		5
9	Price/Sale	Nos		3
10	Price/Book	Nos		3
11	Dividend Payout Ratio	Nos		5
12	Intrinsic Value	Nos		12
Total				**100**

All the students clapped and Prof. Shashank also appreciated the presentation of Ashok and group. Now, it was the turn of Sharon and its team members.

Technical Analysis made easy!

Sharon and her Team had recorded the whole Workshop given by Mr. Kiran Pathak. Sharon played the video . . .

Kiran Pathak welcomed all participants and assured them that they not only will understand how to read Technical Charts but also will be able to apply the same and earn handsome profits from the market.

Kiran Pathak started explaining

Technical analysis is primarily the scientific study of prices. We can say that it is the study of past price and volume data of securities in order to predict the future direction of its price.

The Technical Analysis pre supposes that the security being analyses is actively traded. Like any other method of analysis, the technical analysis is not exact science, rather, its purpose is to predict the future direction that prices are likely to take.

Kiran Pathak started explaining

"The field of technical analysis is based on certain assumptions:

The existence of a tradable security for which there is a reasonable large market.

The price of security at any point of time is sum total of various factors like hope, money, power, recent news, current economic conditions, and perception of market players.

The market movement is not chaotic; rather it has orderly movement in the markets. This suggest that markets generally moves in trends.

Market players tends to repeat their actions over and over again. Technical Analysis therefore holds that the price patterns once identified can be traded effectively since market players are likey to repeat their previous reactions in similar future situations.

Kiran Pathak again said "Now that you understand the philosophy behind technical analysis, we'll get into explaining how it really works. One of the best ways to understand what technical analysis is (and is not) is to compare it to fundamental analysis. We'll do this and then we shall get into depth of the subject".

Kiran Pathak had extraordinary command over his subject. Even though he had no formal qualification to support, he was the master. He had developed various concepts through observation where he challenged several pros and proved them wrong.

His keen observation of stock market and the Charts for 18 years had made him genius.

The Hall which had 30 participants came from different walks of life Some were Stock Traders, few were amateurs, some had come for the first time to understand about stock. Few students were also there. Sharon was like in such a mode that she did not want to miss a single word spoken by the genius She wanted to make maximum use of the opportunity.

The video was on and students were listening to everything very attentively. They had never seen someone so confident about his subject and also being practical at the same time. Mr Pathak was on . . . He said "There is something called Trend. Recently there was Trend everyone wanted to do BE/Btech and then MBA, earlier people wanted to get into Civil Services . . . in the similar fashion

Trend

A trend indicates that there exists an inequality between the forces of supply and demand. When supply of the stock or commodity is greater than the demand for it, the trend will be down since there are more sellers than buyers.

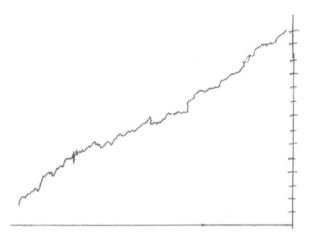

Figure 1

It isn't hard to see that the trend in Figure 1 is up. However, it's not always this easy to see a trend:

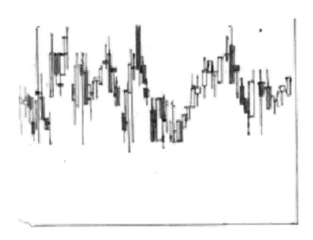

Figure 2

When demand exceeds supply, the trends will be up as the more numerous buyers bid up the price

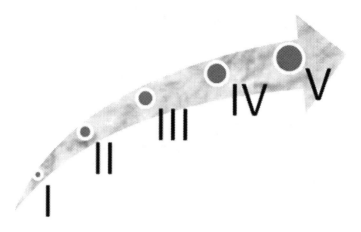

Figure 3

Figure 3 is an example of an uptrend.

And if the forces of supply and demand are nearly equal, the market will move sideways—in what is called a trading range, sideways trends.

Pathak asked "Is there anyone who could not understand the Trend" . . . No was the reply everyone understood it.

Pathak started explaining,

Support And Resistance

A trend line formed by joining the higher lows of an up trend line is also called a support line. These

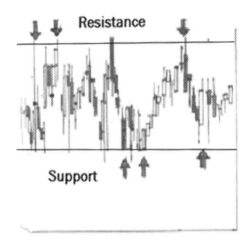

Figure 4

Are the price levels where fresh buying interest comes in which leads to the price bouncing back higher. Prices are likely to find support in the vicinity or around the support trend line.

Conversely, ad down trend line formed by joining the lower highs also act as a resistance line. The price levels along this line are price points where the stock attracts selling pressure.

There was a question "Why Does it Happen?".

Pathak replied "These support and resistance levels are seen as important in terms of market psychology and supply and demand. Support and resistance levels are the levels at which a lot of traders are willing to buy the stock (in the case of a support) or sell it (in the case of resistance)."

But the **Importance of Support and Resistance is that** it can be used to make trading decisions and identify when a trend is reversing. For example, if a trader identifies an important level of resistance that has been tested several times but never broken, he or she may decide to take profits as the security moves toward this point because it is unlikely that it will move past this level.

Pathak was going on smoothly "Now let us understand importance of the Volume.

While price is the primary item of concern in technical analysis, volume is also extremely important.

What is Volume?

Volume, or the number of underlying securities traded, is an important part of the study of price charts. Volume tells us whether or not there is active market interest in the security. Volume however is a relative term. Whether a particular level of volume is high or low depends on the security's normal trading volume, its price, the securitie's inclusion etc.

First of all any price move supported with higher or increasing volume is suggestive of strong trend.

Thus

Rising prices along with rising volumes is abullish sign and Falling prices along with the rising volumes is abearish sign.

Conversely therefore any price move which is not supported by a volume expansion is suggestive of a weak trend. Thus

Rising price accompanied by falling volumes is potentially bearish sign and Falling prices accompanied by falling volumes is a potentially a bullish sign.

Figure: 5

What Is A Chart?

Prices of any security can be plotted on the graph paper in much the same way as we used to make graphs in school. But there are obvious limitations to manual plotting. The graphic representation helps the investor to find out the trend of the price without any difficulty. The charts also have the following uses

Spots the current trend of buying and selling

Indicates the probable future action of the market projection

Shows the past historic movement

Indiactes the important areas of support and resistance.

Chart Based on Time Frame

Daily Charts showing a days open, high, low and closing prices.

Weekly charts showing a week's open, high, low and closing prices. A week is always assumed to start on Monday and end on Friday.

Monthly Charts showing a month's open, high, low and closing prices.

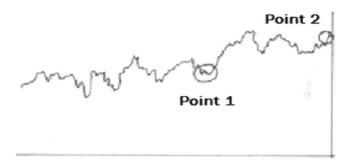

Figure 6

Figure 6 provides an example of a basic chart. It is a representation of the price movements of a stock over a 1.5 year period.

Chart Types

There are three main types of charts that are used by investors and traders. They are: the line chart, the bar chart and the candlestick chart

Line Chart

A Line chart where only the closing price of the day/ period is plotted.

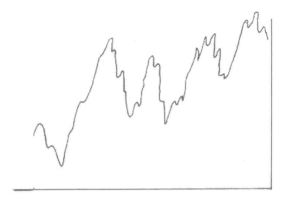

Figure 7: A line chart

Bar Charts

The bar chart_were only the open, high, low and closing prices are plotted in the form of bar.

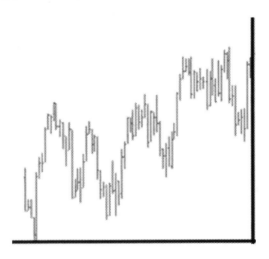

Figure 8: A bar chart

Candlestick Charts

The candlestick chart is where the open, high, low and closing prices are depicted in the form of Japanese Candle stick.

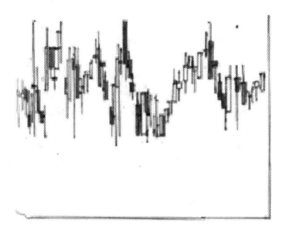

Figure 9: A candlestick chart

Chart Patterns

A Chart patterns are distinctive formations caused by changes in the forces of supply and demand which emerge when prices are plotted on a graph paper or nowadays charted using computer software. These patterns have ameaning which can be interpreted in terms of propable future trend development. What then becomes important is the skill to identify these patterns on the price chart.

Head and Shoulders

Such a price formation occurs after a consistent run up in prices climaxing in a fast and furious non stop price rally, after which the price subsequently makes alower high formation. This is atypical and commonly found price apttern as the climax rally represents irrational optimism before sanily is restored.

Head and Shoulder pattern is figuratively similar to the human form of two shoulders and head. The first shoulder left is formed in continuation of the ongoing up trend. A steep and fast rally then takes the price to new high. Thereafter there is cooling off period during the price retraces to the neckline and subsequently makes a lower high. This is the initial indication that the reversal could be due. The breaking of the neckline is the confirmation of reversal signal.

Inverse Head and Shoulder

This price formation occurs after after a consistent fall in prices, climaxing with afast and furious non stop price crash and finally ending in ahigher low formation. This is atypical price pattern as the panic crash represents extreme human pessism before investors realize that things may not really be quite as bad.

An inverse had and shoulder formation is figuratively the mirror image of ahead and shoulder formation. The first shoulder is formed in continuation with ongoing down trend. Then the steep and fast crash takes price to new low. Thereafter there is some cooling off and prices retraces to the neckline and subsequently make a higher low. This is ainitial indication that a reversal may be due. The breaking of the neckline on the upside is the confirmation of the reversal signal.

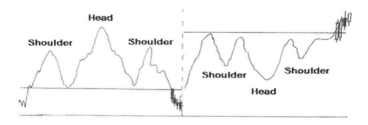

Figure 10: Head and shoulders top is shown on the left. Head and shoulders bottom, or inverse head and shoulders, is on the right.

Pathak said," But the most important part is how to predict to what extent the price will go up or go down. I will tell you the way by which almost upto 80% of you wd be right in predicting".

a. Criteria:
    1. Close above Neck Line
    2. Increase in volume on breakthrough (upto 40%)

If the above criteria is met then we can say it is head and shoulder pattern

b. Calculate X = Low of Head to Neckline
c. Target = Breakout point + X
d. Time = Count Candle from 1st Neck point to breakout/3

Cup and Handle

This is abullish pattern which looks like a cup and handle.

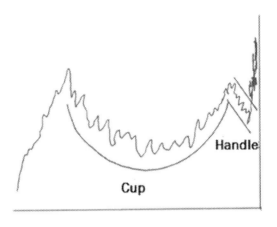

Figure 11

Now How to confirm the pattern.

a. Criteria:
1. Historically Price @ higher band
2. Sharp Fall
3. A spike
4. Price below high of Spike for min—2 yrs
5. Close above High of Spike with increased volume

How to Calculate X

Calculate x	: X = High of Spike
Target	: 5 * X
Time	: Max 2 Years

Double Tops and Bottoms

A double top price pattern forms usually at the end of the consistent rise in the prices whn the price re test a previous high but is unable to go any higher since it finds more sellers than buyers at the previous high level and is thus unable to form a higher high.

A double top formation usually occurs at the end of long up trend. The security's failure to break above the previous high price level and its subsequent move downgrade are suggestive that a new high is not made and therefore the basic premise of an up trend, namely the formation of higher hghs and lower lows is not satisfies. This fact cautions investors and traders that areversal may now be due.

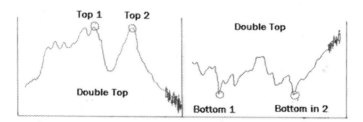

Figure 12: A double top pattern is shown on the left, while a double bottom pattern is shown on the right.

A double bottom formation usually occurs at the end of a long down trend. The security's failure to break below previous low price level and the subsequent move upward suggest and anew low has been made and therefore the basic premise of down trend namely lower highs and lower lows is not satisfied. This fact alerts investors that areversal in the prevailing down trend may now be due.

For Double Bottom the Criteria for confirmation of Formation is

a. Criteria: 1. Equal bottom from same down trend (+—5% Tolerance)
                 2. White Candle after 2nd Bottom with increased volume.

b. Calculate X : Top of Temple—Bottom Line
c. Target   : Bottom Line + x/2 Candle
d. Time   : <u>1st Bottom candle to Next white Candle of next Bottom</u>

Flag and Pennant

Flag is a price formation which occurs diring an ongoing down trend when for a relatively short period price tend to form higher highs coupled with higher lows. However the higher high and higher low formation is not large enough to suggest a reversal in the down trend.

A bearish flag formation indicates that after a consistent fall in price, certain sections of the market are creating buying pressure on the price-hence the higher high formations—but are not successful in convincing the other players of the change in trend.

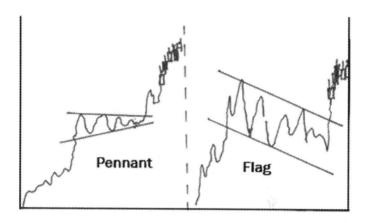

Figure 13

1. Criteria:
    1. Up Move
    2. Consolidation
    3. Closed above consolidation with increased volume

Calculate X	: Length of Pole
Target	: X + Low of Flag
Time	: No of candle from start of Pole to breakthrough / 3

Triple Tops and Bottoms

While the basic reasons for these price patterns and the strategy for trading them remains similar to double top or double bottom formations the triple formations indicates prices have thrice found support at aparticular price level. Conversely a triple top formation indicates that prices have thrice found resistance at a particular price level.

Thus when a security finally confirms a reversal from a triple top or bottom formations one can expect a stronger reversal.

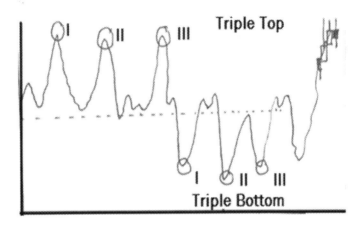

Figure 14

Rounding Bottom

This is a price formation which occurs after a consistent fall in prices. At the later stages of the fall the price fails to make significant lows thiugh the trading interest measured by volumes remains high. Thus the situation becomes one of high volume trading no marked fall in price.

A rounding bottom pattern signaled by high volmes couples with insignificant price movement, is suggestive of slow accumulation taking place.

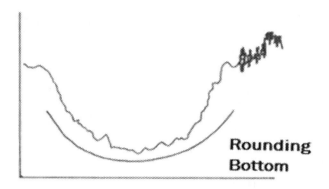

Figure 15

Moving Averages

The three most common types of moving averages are simple, linear and exponential.

Simple Moving Avergae (SMA): This is the most common method used to calculate the moving average of prices. It simply takes the sum of all of the past closing prices over the time period and divide the result by the number of prices used in the calculations.

Linear Weighted Average (LWA): This moving average indicator is the least common out of three and is used to address the problem of the equal weighting. It is calculated by taking the sum of all closing prices over a certain time period and multiplying them by the position of the data point and then dividing by the sum of the number of periods.

Exponential Moving Average (EMA): This moving average calculation uses a smoothing factor to place a higher weight on recent data points and is regarded as much more efficient than the linear weighted average. Having an understanding of the calculation is not generally required cause most charting packages do the calculations.

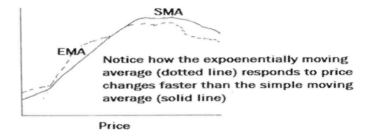

Figure 16

How to use EMA for making Investment Decision:

1. Draw a chart of EMA of 5 day, 13 day and 23 Day.
2. For Short range 20-26 Day EMA is taken.
3. For Longer Range; EMA of 200 Day is taken.

Strategy: Sell 30% when 5 day EMA crosses 13 Day EMA and sell remaining 70% when 5 day EMA Crosses 23 day EMA. Crosses over should be within 3 preceding candles.

Indicators And Oscillators

The distinction between an indicator and Osscillators is that Oscillators are those indicators whose values tends to oscillates between a fixed range usually from 0 to 100.

Thus all indicators are not Oscillators but all oscillators are essentially indicators.

Identifying Overbought and Oversold Market Condtions

The first and foremost use of an indicator is that it reveals whether a price move whether up or down is nearing exhaustion. Oscillators are typically more useful for this purpose but even non oscillating indicators can also detect such sitiations. On oscillatorsvon overbought condition is depicted when the value of the oscillator rise above 75 (in range of 0 to 100). On oscillator oversold condition is depicted when the value of the oscillators falls below 25 (in range of 0 to 100).

Moving Average Convergence Divergence

The MACD is atrend defining indicator. It is not an oscillator as its computation can, theoretically take any value. MACD is calculated as the differenc of two moving averages. This difference is then plotted as the MACD Indicator.

MACD = shorter term moving average—longer term moving average

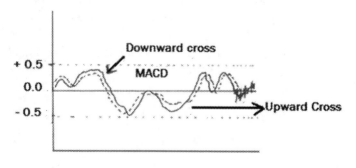

Figure 18

As a trading tool, one may use the MACD for generating buy and sell signals. This can be done by superimposing a moving average line of the MACD itself. When using the standard parameters of 12 DMA and 26DMA, its normal to superimpose a 9 day moving average of the MACD. Thus

A buy signal is generated when the MACD line crosses the signal line—namely the 9 day moving average of MACD—from below. Traders using the method may want to use the filter og buying on the dayafetr the crossover if the prices rises above the signal days high.

A sell signal is generated when the MACD line crosses the signal line from above. Traders using this method for trading may want to use the filter of selling the day after the crossover if the price falls below the signal day's low.

Relative Strength Index

Like RSI any other indicator can be used to give buying and selling signals. The 9 day moving average line of the RSI is superimposed on the RSI line. Crossover of these lines generates the required signals thus

When the RSI line cuts its 9 day average line from below, a buy signal is generated and trader can enter long (buy) the stock.

Conversely when the RSI line cuts its 9 day average line from above, a sell signal is generated and the traders can go short (sell) the stock.

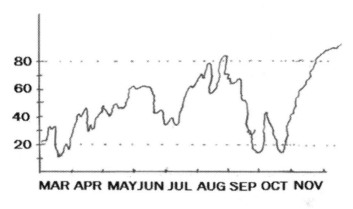

Figure 19

Stochastic Oscillator

Invented by George Lane the stochastic indicator is an oscillator which tries to measure the relative position of the closing price usually at the end of a day or any pre defined period. To be more precise, it tracks whether the day or the selected periods closing price was nearer to the days low or nearer the days high.

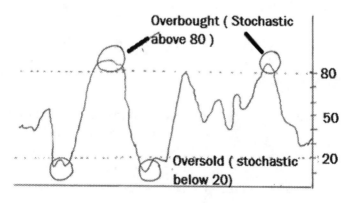

Figure 20

When the closing price is nearer the days low instead of nearer the day's high during an up trend or when in a down trend the closing orice is nearer the high (rather than days low), it is warning to the trader that the ongoing move is growing weak.

The indicator tries to track this mood in the form of a graph.

Meanwhile someone from the audience asked "Is there any quantitative method to confirm and decide on a particular stock about its investment worthiness?".

Pathak replied, "Yes". We call it Risk to reward ratio. We recommend it to be at least 1:3 i.e. incase someone is ready to take Risk which is 1 than three times of the risk, he should get the reward. Let me explain you with example

Example :

Close: 500 Stop Loss:475 Target:650

Risk = Cost Price — Stop Loss => 500 — 475 = 25

Reward = Target — Cost Price => 650 — 500 = 150

Risk: Reward

25: 150 => 1: 6. It should be minimum 1:3. Here in this case it is 1:6 so it's fairly good stock to invest.

We need to ensure that we make more Profit and less Loss, that was the concluding remarks of Mr. Pathak.

The recorded video was over, professor along with the students were satisfied by the presentation and the amount of knowledge they have gained through this lecture cum session of Mr. Pathak. And bell rung.

Well this was the end of the lecture and for the day as well, for from the next day onwards they had diwali vacations. All the students gave greetings to their favorite professors, they wished them happy diwali, few gave greeting cards . . . sweets, and some invited their professors for the Diwali Party . . . . they also wished each other happy Diwali and with the sweet note they all dispersed. Nisaa, Ashok, Sharon, Kapil, Chhabi and Vihaan . . . they have become a group now. They all hugged and wished each other the Happy Diwali.

Fun with 'Derivatives'

Diwali vacations were over . . . all were back . . . they distributed sweets and prashad to all the teachers, to their friends and even to the canteen guy. Canteen was again filled with same hustle and bustle. Students were chirping and transferring their diwali pics to their friends' mobiles through whats app, Bluetooth, some put them on the facebook as well. Hence they all were very happy to show their new shopping, they did in their home town and thus they all were busy . . . and soon the bell rang . . . .

They all rushed towards the classroom, as they knew if they are late then they won't be allowed to enter the classroom. Fortunately all reached the classroom and they felt themselves lucky that the professor was late so they weren't caught getting late. And here enters the Professor Shashank, students immediately stood to give him a corporate clap, but . . . . suddenly they all stopped one by one . . . they all were shocked to see their professor, there was murmuring in the classroom . . . . students were doubtful if he is their Professor, Sharon, Nisaa, Vihaan, Kapil, Chhabi, Ashok all were shocked to see their professor in this situation.

Professor Shashank, who was the most fit, dynamic, energetic and vibrant faculty, stood in front of them as a very weak, thin. Today again he was in full sleeved shirt and his blazer though he tried his level best to look smart but, his dull and pale face, sunken eyes, dry lips described some other story. His usual brightness in eyes were missing. A musty odour was accompanied by his breath. He was reduced to half but he had bulging belly, that gave him look of a fat person, for which he made useless efforts to hide them through his blazer. He looked extremely tired and diseased. He looked extremely worn-out.

He interrupted the students' thoughts by asking them, "How was your diwali vacations?"

All the students replied slowly, "Fine sir" with a dull tone.

He started, "So, today we will study about the derivatives . . ." "In fact we will learn how to invest in derivatives?"

Suddenly Ashok asked, "Sir, what is the time period for which we need to make investment?" "Didn't you attend my lecture when i had talked about various time frame for which you can invest?" Professor replied in a bit annoyance. This was the first time he became angry with someone. Ashok kept quiet.

"Ok, I will explain again:

Short Term: Days to few Months
Mid term: Couple of years
Long term: More than 8-10 years or so.

Generally for amateurs who don't have much experience in stock market should not go for short term investment but need to stay for at least couple of years or more than that."

Today when everyone was in silent mode, Ashok was in form. He kept on asking question, "Sir it's fine but is there any way by which we can get returns, i mean more returns but In less time?"

"Yes there is a way, it is called Derivatives. By this way you can earn more returns in Short time. But it is slightly more speculative in nature and the investor has to speculate the trend and the price to which the stock may go."

Suddenly Sharon joined the discussion and asked, "But Sir I read somewhere Warren Buffet had said that "Derivatives are financial weapons of mass destruction."

Professor laughs with a bit difficulty kept his hand on chest while doing so "Yes he is right if u get into the same without proper knowledge. It is similar to giving Gun in the hands of Monkey. But if the Gun is in the hand of a trained person, he can use it efficiently and judiciously. So don't worry what he says if you have knowledge and thirst to learn more and become expert, you can mint money."

By the time Kapil has also regained his senses and he also joined them, because he knew professor shall be satisfied if they will ask more questions, "Sir it's looking interesting but also confusing can you tell us in detail."

He was right and the professor became glad that students are participating in his lecture, he immediately said

"Sure, Derivatives are financial instruments which derive their value from their underlying assets or securities.

For example if buyers enter into a contract with seller to buy specific number of shares of a company at a specified price after a specified period, the buyer has entered into a future contract. It is important to note that the buyer is buying the contract and not the stock of shares under reference. This contract is called Derivatives while the stock of shares to which it applies is called underlying asset. Apart from future other commonly used derivatives are options, convertibles, swaps and warrants to name a few."

"So, is it only stock which is the underlying asset?" asked Ashok in declarative way.

"No" professor replied firmly, "The underlying assets can be securities, commodities, bullion, precious metals, currency, live stock and index such as interest rates and exchange rates."

"And sir what do the derivatives do?" asked Vihaan. Professor was now fully charged by the interaction of his students, "Well, Derivatives attempt either to **minimize the loss** arising from adverse price movements of the underlying asset or **maximize the profits** arising out of favorable price fluctuation. Since derivatives derive their value from the underlying asset they are called as derivatives. Based on the underlying assets derivatives are classified into: (sharing the slide)

a) Financial Derivatives (UA: Fin asset)
b) Commodity Derivatives (UA: gold etc)
c) Index
d) Derivative (BSE sensex)."

Ashok who sat on the first bench made a confusing expression and started doing hair itching . . . which made professor understood that he couldn't understand. He said, "Ok, I will explain this to you again."

He added, "See, Derivatives are basically **risk shifting** instruments. Hedging is the most important aspect of derivatives and also their basic economic purpose. Derivatives can be compared to an insurance policy. As one pays premium in advance to an insurance company in protection against a specific event, the derivative products have a payoff contingent upon the occurrence of some event for which he pays premium in advance."

Suddenly Ashok again asked, "And sir i have heard about term options, what are these?" "Good question, Well, options are one of the type of derivatives instrument." Professor said, "I will tell you about all the derivatives instruments. They are:

Forward contracts
Futures
Commodity
Financial (Stock index, interest rate & currency)
Options :Put and Call
Swaps.
Interest Rate
Currency"

Professor added (while sharing the slide) "Now Let me explain you each derivative Instruments." Students were more attentive.

Futures:

A future contract is essentially a serrieds of contracts. There are three types of people who deal in future:

Speculators Speculator buy and sell futures for the sole purpose of marketing a profit by selling them at price that is higher than their buying price. Such people neither produce nor use the asset in the ordinary course of business.

Hedgers: In contrast, they buy and sell futures to offset an otherwise risky position in the spot market in ordinary coutrse of business, they either produce or use asset.

Arbitrageurs: They gain from the price differentiation of different markets.

In this contract the trader who promises to buy is said to be in "Long Position" and one who promises to sell is in" Short Position". The Long position is afuture contract is the agreement to take delivery and short position in a future contract is the legally binding agreement to deliver.

How one makes money in Future

The long makes money when the underlying assets price rises above the futures price.

The short makes money when the underlying asset's price falls below the futures price.

Professor became exhausted sat on the chair and added, "Besides these there is another way by which you can earn handsome returns and the instrument is more evolved and has better security arrangements. Let me explain you with a case study.

Professor gave a conceptual speech on "Options are (sharing the slide)

An option is a contract which gives the buyer the right, but not the obligation, to buy or sell an underlying asset at a specific price on or before a certain date.

Options Lingo

Underlying: This is the underlying asset.

Option Premium: It is the price paid by the buyer to the seller to acquire the right to buy or sell the asset. It is the total cost of an option.

Strike Price or Exercise Price :price of an option which is pre-determined price of the underlying asset on or before the expiration day.

Expiration date: The date on which the option expires.

Exercise Date: is the date on which the option is actually exercised.

European style of options: Here buyer can exercise his option only on the expiration day & not anytime before that.

American style of options: Here it can be excercised on or before the expiration date.

Call option: It gives the owner the **right to buy** an specified amount of underlying security at a specified price within a specified time.

Put Option: It gives owner the right to sell a specified amount of an underlying security at a specified price within a specified time.

Positions

Long Position: The term used when a person owns a security and he is bullish on the security and wants to sell.

Short position: The owner is bearish on the security and expect it to go down and the term describe the selling of a security, commodity, or currency. Here the the investor's sales exceed holdings cause he believe the price will fall.

Thus professor kept on dictating and telling them about the various concepts. Some students were attentive, some were hesitant to ask questions, some were thinking about him and thus the lecture got over. The professor said bye and left the classroom with satisfaction and smile as usual, though today his smile lacked usual symphony.

As the professor left the classroom, immediately all the students gathered and started discussing about the professor's health. They were really worried about the professor. They were talking about his appearance, some said he had fever, some said perhaps he is not well . . . but no one was able to guess what exactly was the problem. At last Sharon, Kapil, Ashok, Chhabi, Vihaan and few more students decided to visit the professor's place. And they all dispersed for the day.

Secrets of Life

All the students reached the professor's flat . . . It was a 2bhk flat . . . They rang the bell and the door was opened by a young boy of approx 19-20 years, black eyes, black properly combed hair, dark complexion and height of about 5'5".

"Yes??" he said.

"We are professor's student students, came to meet him." Said Kapil. "To ask some questions . . . ." added Sharon and they looked at each other.

"Well, but the sahib is not at home, he has gone to see the doctor."

"it's Ok, we will wait for him . . ." all said in unison.

The boy permitted them to enter the room. It was the well furnished room with all the amenities . . . at the entrance there was a big idol of Lord Ganesh on the wall and in one corner there was a shoe stand which was neatly kept. Through the entrance one can easily see the kitchen, and the other two rooms which were also properly managed. Everything was kept in place . . . the flat was too tidy. In the living room there was a sofa set one side, all the students sat there, a couch on the other side, a 21 inch plasma TV on opposite side of the wall, a deewan with a rajasthani designs in left corner. There was a lobby attached to the living room and it had many plants and pots with different types of flowers. Chhabi could not resist herself to go in the lobby, and soon she was there, looking at the sunset, birds, river flowing beneath, flowers in the lobby. The view was really mesmerizing.

The boy brought the cold drinks and few snacks for all of them. All said thanks and took it. The boy sat on the couch next to the sofa. Sharon asked him his name, he said, "Raghu".

"So, Raghu do you study?" asked Kapil, taking a sip.

"Yes, am doing graduation from a commerce college. it's only due to grace of Sahab that i got admission into it, else i didn't have a single penny to do anything. He is a very nice person. But . . ." Raghu's voice was crumpling.

Suddenly Vihaan asked, "What happened dear, why are you getting emotional? Didn't you get good marks?"

"No, sir not at all. Its not about that . . . It's something very serious . . . It's about professor"

"What?" all got shockingly curious. Raghu was silent for a while. They all became alert. "Please Raghu tell us what is it?"

"Sir is suffering from some disease, though he never told me about it. But there is something serious and he won't live for long" Raghu started sobbing.

Students were shocked to hear this. They were not able to believe over what they heard. They all sank. "Are you sure? How can you say that? I mean, you might be wrong also . . ." Sharon said with crumpling voice.

"No, this is true, because he telling me very often like, do this do that before i go, he also called the lawyer for the will and he says, will hardly live for 6-7 months."

There was a silence in the room. Everyone was motionless . . . wordless . . . . they were shivered and cut to pieces just by the thought of it. "We have to do something, before it gets too late." Suddenly said Sharon. She had decided that this time she won't allow death to win over her. She decided that anyhow she will save her professor by any means. "Yes!! definitely" all said in unison. "We will not allow this to happen to our favourite professor. We all owe our life to him and now it's the time to give him back . . . what he gave to us . . ."

"Who is his doctor? Where is his hospital?" Kapil immediately shouted at Raghu. "I will give you his visiting card, I had one" Raghu went inside and brought one.

"Thank you soo much . . . . you have helped us a lot." Kapil said to Raghu.

"Its okk, sir. Thats all i can do."

"No, dear . . . You are the biggest help to him . . . you are serving a great man, an ideal professor, none of us got that opportunity. You are doing a noble work. God bless you." Sharon said.

"I need blessings for my sahib, that's it . . ." Raghu 's eyes were moist.

"Don't worry dear . . . we will try our best." Vihaan added.

"Let's go to the doctor . . . only he can guide us . . ." Kapil said and all nodded in unison.

They were about to leave, when Ashok said to Raghu, "Hey boss, i have a request, don't tell professor about us being here . . ."

"Sure, not at all . . ." said Raghu and smiled.

They all came out of the society and looked at the visiting card. Kapil was the localized amongst all, so he decided to read the address.

"Dr. Naveen Salunke, Gastro Liver Specialist, M.D. (Medicine), D.M. (Gastroenterologist), Trained in Therapeutic Endoscopy at Hamburg, Germany Clinical Observer Harvard Medical School, Boston, USA"

"Seems a great one!!" Sharon said.

"Yups and his clinic is OMG . . . in Vishrantwadi . . ." Kapil said.

"Why? What happened?" asked Ashok.

"Its too far . . ."

"Well, that's not a problem, we can go anywhere for our professor . . ." said everyone in unison.

"Yes, you all are right. So, i think only few of us should go and rest of you can go back to hostel. We will let you know about the status."

"Okzz . . . . I will come with you." said Sharon immediately before anyone can say this. "No, we will also go, why only you . . ." other students said.

"Look, firstly we don't have other conveyance except my car . . . you all came by bus and Vishrantwadi is too far . . . by car it may take 2-3 hours and we will reach there by 7pm and again return journey means another 2 hours so it will be approx 10-11pm. So better you all go . . . chill i will give you all the details." Kapil said in an elderly voice.

"Ok, as you say . . ." And rest of the students left for the hostel.

It was 5:30p.m. Sharon and Kapil sat in Kapil's car and they started moving towards the doctor's place in Vishrant wadi. Kapil drew fast . . . He saw Sharon sitting beside him. She was in green colored chinos, black colored shirt and black colored shoes. Her hair as usual was flowing on her face. She looked pretty. Kapil was happy to be with her. Its long they have spent time together alone. But he didn't talk much as he can clearly see the tension on Sharon's face, she was worried about professor. There was weariness in her eyes, she was struggling with her fist, and wanted to reach the hospital as soon as possible. After about one hour of observation, he broke the silence and just asked her, "Are you okay?"

"Yes . . . but"

"I understand, relax . . . . we will do something."

"We have to . . ." said Sharon in a voice which had mixed emotions.

"Well we have reached Vishrantwadi area . . . Can you please dictate me the address?"

"Yeah sure, it is . . . Dr. Navin Salunke 's Clinic, Near Dhanori Post Office, Pune, Maharashtra—411015" reading out from the visiting card.

"Ok . . . so next we have to find out where is Dhanori . . ."

Sharon enquired from few people about Dhanori and searching, asking, they ultimately reached Dhanori post office and in no time they found the Dr. Salunke's Clinic.

Kapil parked the car in front of the clinic and they stepped out of the car. Sharon and Kapil both were too nervous to talk about the Professor's disease. Both of them were nervous and afraid. It was 8:32pm. It took almost two hours to reach there. The clinic was still open and there was a long queue in the dispensary. The people from different background stood there. Few were villagers, localities, some from rich families and few like them who came to enquire about their near ones. It looked so weird that in front of life and death there is no financial inequality, all are treated equally, no matter what is your status. This is the harsh truth of life, Someone has rightly said that no one carries anything to heaven, everything is left behind.

They stood in the queue but it would have taken much time had Kapil not gone to the nurse to get special favour. He went to the receptionist and handed over her a Rs. 500 note and she fixed the appointment in the second place. Well, this made Kapil to feel that money matters, one should know how to use it. Though he knew Sharon won't like it and he was right, she stared at Kapil . . . and said with annoyance, "Every time you need to do this?"

He preferred to be silent then to argue her because he knew they are different from one another. And here came the appointment, Kapil got an opportunity to boast off, "Look this is because of me". Sharon made a dirty gesture, "huh!!". Kapil thought "What's the problem with girls, why they are so impractical, let it be."

They were inside the cabin . . . Dr Salunke sat there on his chair with a towel on the back of chair. The whole office was on the blue theme. There were books on gastro, livers and many others, name were too difficult to remember. The office was nicely decorated with all scientific and biological stuff. On one side of the table was a light lamp, stethoscope and a notepad and pen. He asked both of them, "Yes" and pointed towards the chair. They sat on the chair in front of his table.

Sharon started, "Sir, actually we are students of IIAMS college. Me Sharon and he is Kapil, my friend. We came to talk about our professor Mr. Shashank. He is a regular patient in your clinic and recently we came to know that he is suffering from something serious." She added hesitatingly "And we want to know wats dat."

"Look dear i cannot tell about the history of my patient to anyone."

"Sir, please, u know that he is on death bed, don't u want him to live, don't you want your patient should stay alive?. We just want to help him." She became impatient. "He is more than a professor to all of us. Please sir try to understand. Lets we all should try our level best to save him and i know together we can do this." Kapil added. "Yes sir, please" Sharon too added.

"It's too late now. We cannot do anything."

Sharon and Kapil sank, "What do u mean sir?"

"Actually he is suffering from Liver cirrhosis, last stage of it. At this stage the liver is completely damaged and no medicine can work on it. Gradually he loses his weight, his memory, concentration power, his health, his body, will decline."

"I still wonder how he manages to take lectures. Am sorry to say but he has life of maximum 6-7 months." Both started staring each other, now they could recollect every incident where Professor had behaved absent mindedly, has coughed, looked confused and in some other world. They could make out meaning of those signals now.

"So, what u want to say, there is no other way to save him?" Sharon almost cried.

"No, i didn't mean that, but . . . ."

"But, what doctor . . . please tell can we do anything for him. Please tell."

"Liver transplant, the only option left."

"We will do it . . . Where, how much, how, when . . . . ? Please tell everything, we will do it."

"Its not easy dear, this transplantation costs approx 30 lakhs in India and about 60 lakhs outside India. But the survival rate is again doubtful."

"How?"

"In India the survival rate is generally 60-70 percent but in abroad it is 97%. So, u can see how risky is this?"

"Have you told professor about it?"

"Yes, but he doesn't have money for this operation and he chose death."

"Sir please guide us, how to go about it?"

"Look i have contacts in Delhi, I can arrange . . ."

"No, not in Delhi . . . the best in the world where they have maximum survival rate. We want there."

"Are you sure? The amount is big."

"Sir, you just do preparation for his surgery, we will arrange the money."

"Ok, the best is in US, I will make all the arrangements from my side. All the best."

"Thank u doctor. (Passing on her visiting card to doctor) Last favour sir, please don't tell professor that we were here." Kapil was surprised to see that Sharon has her visiting card also.

"A broker!!" looking at the visiting card "Sure" said doctor and smiled.

Kapil was shocked and confused to listen the word broker, but perhaps that wasn't the correct time to discuss about it. They came out of the cabin and moved towards the parking lot.

"Don't you think 60 lakhs is a big amount?" Kapil said.

"Yes, it is"

"So, how you will do it?"

"It's not just me, WE will do it."

Kapil unlocked the car and they both sat in it. "But together how can we do this? . . . ." He started the car and the car was now moving towards the destination.

"Don't worry, we will find a way. I just don't want to lose one more person in my life and for that I can do anything."

"ONE MORE?"

"Nothing . . ." Sharon took a bottle of water and gulped few. Kapil stared at her face. Her nose was red, her voice was heavier . . . he understood . . . that she is about to cry. He stopped the car in front of a hotel, remembering the last mishap, this time he made a safe move. He asked, "What happened, are you okay?"

"No, nothing is okay."

"Don't worry, we will save our professor and you said no? that we all will do it . . . together . . ."

"But, why me? always, why me?"

"What?"

"Why does the destiny always do this to me, why i always have to lose my near and dear ones?" She almost broke, her frustration, anger, grief all was visible at a time.

"What are you talking? Am not getting you?"

"No, you will never understand"

"Why? Am i not ur friend. Cm on you can tell me." Kapil held Sharon's shoulders.

"Nothing, i am just too unlucky for those who love me . . . . or to say whom I love." Kapil guessed whether he falls in any of the two categories.

"I don't know what does the life wants from me. I . . . . wat shud i do . . . i am good for nothing . . ." Sharon just broke herself into his arms. She was sobbing. She felt so protective after long. Kapil held her tightly and just tried to console her. He didn't understand what had happened that made her say like this. He wanted to ask her, what was she talking about, but he felt better to console her than to ask. For a moment Kapil felt so great that Sharon was in his arms. This was the moment for which he has waited so long. Her hair was coming on his face. He can smell her odour and his lips touched her forehead. He kissed her on her forehead. Sharon was still in his arms unperturbed by his kiss. Perhaps she didn't notice it, but her silence gave courage to Kapil to proceed further. He just took her face into his cupped hands. Sharon's eyes were moist, she was crying and she was just silently looking into the eyes of Kapil. Her eyes were sad, lonely and in pain. She was not in a situation to figure out anything. But, Kapil couldn't resist himself. He kissed on her eyes and sucked her tears. Sharon just closed her eyes, she didn't protest. Kapil kissed her on her both cheeks and he touched her soft lips and put his lips, that were moistened by tears. On hers. He kissed her softly, gently, slowly and she was still silent. Sharon almost laid on him as if she got someone on whom she can rely, for that moment she forgot everything, for a moment she realised, was with someone to whom she can give her feelings, emotions, soul and body. There was a feel of care, affection which she wanted for long, which she got from Kapil. She drowned herself into him, but suddenly she realised the truth and she pushed him back with force. She hurriedly opened the door and went out of the car. Kapil was shocked at her sudden reaction, though he expected this much before. He too went out of the car and followed her and just held her hands, "Sharon, please listen to me."

"Please, leave my hands, Kapil."

"I want to say something."

"I don't want to listen anything."

"Please give me one chance. I want to confess something. Please for God's sake."

Sharon was silent this time. Perhaps this was her silent permission. Suddenly Kapil said, "I Love You".

Sharon was shocked to hear those three words from him. She gave a taunting smile, "You love me, really?"

"Yes. I love you very much. I can do anything for you."

"What do you know about me? Do you know about my past? Do you know about my family? Do you know wat i do all the time? Do you know What I am? Nothing, no? Then how can you fall in love with someone whom you don't even know?"

"Love doesn't need any introduction."

"Leave it, Kapil don't waste yours and my time. This philosophy will not work with me. My life is already very complicated and don't make it more complicated. No chance, so better we shouldn't discuss about it anymore. Let's go." She went straight into the car.

Sharon's voice was so firm that Kapil couldn't speak a word and he too went into the car and moved towards her home. They didn't say a single word, in the whole journey of 1:30 hours. Those one and a half hours of silence was like a punishment to Kapil. He felt perhaps he was too early to say those three words. But one thing that struck his mind was the past of Sharon. He decided that he will ask Nisaa about it. He dropped Sharon, she didn't utter a word, while going. Kapil initiated the conversation and said, "Goodnight" She replied, "Same to you" without turning back. After dropping Sharon at about 11:30pm he too reached his home. The servant opened the door, parents were asleep, so he went straight into his room. He was hungry so he went into the kitchen to search for something to eat in the fridge and found pudding and fruit juice, he took few chips as well and went back to his room. He sat on his comfortable bed, eating and thinking about Sharon. It was about 12:00am, but still he could not stop himself from calling Nisaa. He called her thrice and she picked the call in the third time.

"Hello, whose this?" Nisaa said in a sleepy voice.

"Hii"

"Yes, Kaps. You called me so late its . . . . oh yes 12:00. Anything urgent? . . ." "Oh u went to the doctor. right? How was it? What did the doctor say?" Suddenly her voice became normal and conscious.

"That i will tell you later, but right now I want to talk about Sharon . . ."

"What? I mean what about Sharon? She is your junior, or a bright junior, who studies with us but more intelligent than us, that's it . . ."

"I mean i want to know something else."

"What?" Nisaa pretended to act.

"You know wat i mean"

"I really don't know, wat u mean . . ."

"Look, if you won't tell me anything, i won't talk to you anymore . . . I promise u, I swear" the trick worked.

"Now this is so . . . ridiculous . . ."

"Yes, so please tell me about her . . . please"

"Though she didn't want anything to be discussed but said" but promise you won't tell about it to anyone."

"Pakka . . . pakka . . . sure . . ."

Nisaa recalls the day when Sharon had told her everything about her past . . . . she started narrating everything as it is:

"What??? Are you nuts?? U r married . . . .!!!" Nisaa said in surprise.

"Was . . . ." said Sharon

"Means"

"He expired a few months back." Tears trickled down her face. "Yes my bad fate had sucked me, when i lost the most important part of my life, my husband. We got married on 24th Feb, 2011 the best day of my life when i got everything I wished for, i prayed for, in form of my husband, my Viraat, Viraat . . . I felt myself the happiest person on earth . . . the luckiest person on earth . . . My happiness knew no bounds . . . .

Life passed like dreadful night,
U came in life as a Knight . . . .
U crowned my life,
By making me ur wife . . . .

I will keep on loving u more than me,
For u r in life as an angel to me . . .
I miss u incredibly wen v r apart, regardless of
distance v r far . . .
My love might smtym make u astonished, but sorry
for am not yet finished . . .
I love because i love,
I love in order I love . . . .
I love u, I love u,
N I love u this much . . . .

I loved him so much and he loved me even more. I was a kind of arrogant and stubborn girl but only he was the one who knew me better than me. We never had a fight, he knew how to control me as if I was a lock and he was the master key. We were made for each other. We spent time together, made plans for the future. He was always favoured me to go of higher studies. He was in corporate but he never forced me to be a part of the corporate, because he knew about mutual funds, shares, investments are something which fascinated me. Someone has correctly said that "Opposites attract each other". We were completely different. He was shy and i was extrovert, he never believed in PDA (Public Display Of Affection) but i believed this is something to express, he was quiet and i was talkative, he loved to spend more time with me at home and i used to ask him what if we shall spend time together on mountain or near rivers means i was fond of travelling and he was not . . . . he was too matured for me, he had to take care of me all the time like my lunch, my medicines, he use to wake me up early in the morning so that i can go for the meeting early. Being getting up late most of the times i skip my breakfast. But he used to prepare it for me so that i won't be hungry, i take a glass of milk in morning, if it gets too hot he would make it cold by putting the glass of milk in the water, he drops me till the bus stand so that i shouldn't miss my bus, he always kept watch on me if am getting thin . . . . if he observes so he used to fill the refrigerator with fruits so that i shouldn't lose my weight or get weaker . . . he was there with me always in at all times. If i make a cal dat am nt feeling well, he would immediately come and take me to the hospital, he never took me for granted . . . ."

Sharon's eyes were continuously flowing . . . . Nisaa was stunned and didn't stop her . . . .

"After one year, we were blessed with a baby. Viraat was so happy, his happiness knew no bounds on being awarded as a new post of Father. He kissed me and said i have given him the best gift. Till this moment everything went good (delete good, insert well) but no one was aware that soon my life will be eclipsed."

"It started with the sudden death of my baby after one month of his birth. I still remember, he was lying on bed like all innocent babies my 'ansh' was there on bed . . . i was thinking, when he will wake up and start crying for the milk . . . the mother inside me was crying . . . . dying . . . cursing . . . pleading . . . . to all the powers of the world to get back her child . . . . but no one could do anything . . . her every plead . . . every request was in vain . . . there was no one to listen to a mother's voice . . . I was broke . . . this was first experience of my life when I lost someone, so near to me, to death . . . I never ever before had experienced that feeling . . ." "But still I was then in comparatively better situation . . . because I had a loving husband who was ready to do anything for me and my smile. My Viraat was the one who also cried with me but not at loss of baby, but on loss of my happiness, my smile. He was sad on my losses and at any cost he wanted my smile back. He tried everything, he took me on a trip, he then loved me even more than before, he cared me more than ever.

He dropped his lashes, when I felt shy . . .
He gave me sky, when I wished to fly . . . .
He shared his pillow, for my sound sleep . . .
He offered his shoulder, when I weeped . . .
He held my hands, when I felt alone . . .
He accompanied me, when I faced storm . . .
He provided me shade, when I was in rain . . .
He loved me more, when I was in pain . . .
He soothes me, when I was in bright sun . . .
The day he entered my life, it turns to frolic and fun . . .
I know he will never leave me, in this life . . .
For I know I am much more to him, than his wife . . .
He cared me more than I do, He loved me more than I do . . .
I owe my all to him, I wanna spend my whole life with him . . .

When he found his all efforts were in vain, one day he took a promise from me, "Sonu, do u love me?" I said yes then he said," If u really love me then u have to promise me that you will never cry again for 'Ansh'." This promise was a bit hard for me but no doubt I love my Viraat unconditionally, so i made the promise. That was the day, since then I never cried for my baby in front of him. I always tried to keep myself happy, though sometimes I get emotional for my 'Ansh' but I never expressed in front of Viraat. Whenever we go for shopping or any outing whenever I saw any baby, my heart suddenly dump down and tears automatically come in my eyes. My pain was in my heart, which was unknown to anyone . . . this was something which was with me . . . i never knew what he feels, neither he never asked me how i feel on this matter . . . because ultimately we both wanted smile on each other's faces and hence never discussed about 'Ansh' openly . . . but i was still in that pain . . . maybe he was too. After all he was most happy on being a father. But perhaps men are emotionally stronger than women . . . so he managed to hide his pain from me."

"No one knew God wanted me to bear that pain so that i can get strength for the biggest pain which was yet to come in my life . . . ."

"This wasn't the end of my adversities. One year passed after the mishap and now I was emotionally and physically as well in a better condition. We had overcome the pains of our hearts and were busy in our daily routine. We celebrated two years of our marriage anniversary on 24rth Feb, 2013. I was also performing well at my workplace and had plans for higher studies as well and he was extremely good at work. He was selected for onsight programme and we had planned to leave for U.S. by the end of month of May 2013. Everything was going well. Life was still beautiful because I was blessed with the most loving husband on the earth."

"And here arrived the doom's day of my life. It was Monday, 20th May, 2013. I reached home quite early and was busy in my official work. Suddenly bell rang and it was my Viraat at the door. As usual i hugged him and kissed him and took his bag from him and he came inside the room to change. But today he wasn't looking well. His face was dull and donno why he was looking a bit upset. His voice had no symphony, i tried to ask him but he didn't say anything. Then i thought to try something else. I went to the kitchen and prepared his favourite dishes for dinner. Those were 'baigan ka bharta, kheer, jeerarice, dal makhani and roti' and i kept it surprise, as alike all days, today he was busy in watching television instead of coming to kitchen and playing with me which was his usual habit. Though today i tried to play with him, we played badminton and also cracked jokes on myself, shared stupid incidents of my office to make him lighter and to some extent I was successful and now he was singing and voluntarily doing ball dance with me. He was now smiling and the glow of his face which was missing few minutes back, was again visible on his face. By the time my dinner was ready and we had dinner together. He was quite impressed by the dishes i made and gave me a sweet kiss on my cheek. He enjoyed them and i enjoyed watching him smiling. Really I and my life was incomplete without him and his smile, i just thanked God for giving me Viraat as my husband and wished i should never had to spend my life without him. I just can't imagine my life without him."

Sharon's voice was crumpling while speaking further, she couldn't hold back her tears, her eyes were red in rage, frustration, irritation, regrets . . . so many emotions at a time . . . that they were difficult to express. Anyhow she recollected her energy to tell the hardest truth.

"It was 5 a.m., 21st May, 2013 . . . . He had some work to do so, Viraat woke up early than usual, he felt thirsty and went to drink water. Then he felt a slight pain in his chest, he went again and drank luke warm water, perhaps he thought it was due to gas . . . But then also his slight pain continued . . . When he was unable to do anything, he woke me up at about 6:00am. Perhaps he thought I could do something, and I was the biggest fool on earth. On that day I came to know that I was good for nothing. In place of taking him to doctor, i also thought that perhaps it was due to gas and gave him lemon water, which for few minutes worked and he was ok, after drinking it and his pain also gone. I smiled to him as if I did it, I was able to cure him . . . Perhaps my destiny felt like a loser and in no time it reverted back. Viraat again got a pain in his heart and it increased gradually and suddenly he fainted."

"I ran towards him and was unable to understand what to do, then I realized "It could be heart attack" also. I ran to my neighbour to call her for I need to take him to the hospital. I knocked their door, shouted, cried and requested to please take my Viraat to the doctor. My neighbour, along with her husband, came with me. Viraat was lying on the bed. Tears were coming out of his eyes and he was ulti saansein le rhe the. I can feel the pain he has to bear and i was unable to do anything. If i would have been at his place he would have snatched me from the hands of yamraj also, but it was me who was the most unlucky, irresponsible, a loser who was unable to save her child and today was about to lose her husband . . . . and cannot help it . . .

"We immediately took him on a blanket and carried him to a car and reached the nearest hospital in 10 minutes. Viraat was attended by the emergency ward . . . He was taken to the ICU and a panel of doctors were attending him. It was approx 6:50am., there was a weird silence in the hospital, everything was so stable and constant for a moment . . . there was a killing silence like something is going to happen. I was numb what to do my brain was not working, I was quiet, my eyes were dry and stuck to the door of ICU, my thoughts were blocked, my hands and body was getting cold, i felt like anything, ..."

"After about an hour doctors came out of the ICU, I was looking at them but couldn't gather courage to ask them that what happened to my Viraat, is he ok?, shall i take him back to home, shall i meet him? Is he calling me 'sonu'? Can I now see the smile on his face? Will he be able to talk to me? I was just busy in choosing my words, suddenly doctor came to me and said We are sorry."

". . . ."

"Those three words, i couldn't react, i couldn't cry, i was blank, there was darkness in front of my eyes, i . . . i . . . . just said NOOOO . . . . this can't happen to me . . . . I cried and shouted at the doctors, what the hell you are doing, forcibly I went into the ward . . . . my Viraat was lying on the bed . . . his face was so calm and quiet as if he was sleeping and will suddenly wake up and say sonu i was joking . . . I kept on looking at him . . . I held his hand and sat beside him . . . there were no tears in my eyes . . . there was no emotion on my face . . . . no words to scream . . . still was in a delusion is it true or i have a bad dream. My body was unable to balance my weight . . . I ran out of my words . . . The only thought that came in my mind was i can't live without Viraat and also have to go with him . . . I went to my neighbour friend and requested her that i want to go back home, she said to me to wait for few minutes . . . I said to myself . . . no . . . before he leave me forever i have to accompany him . . . . I went towards the washroom and found a gallon of some acid, in no time I took the gallon and started drinking it. I fainted and fell down. Yes, I had wanted to commit suicide but perhaps it's not in the hands of anyone . . . soon I was treated and was hospitalized for few days . . . . I was given medicinal treatment but I felt myself as a loser, everyday I thought of some new ways to commit suicide . . . I had nothing, no one whom i can take care of. I was the person who had lost everything to death and have no purpose to live, no desire to live, no wishes, no dreams, no demands all i wanted was I want to go back to my Viraat . . ."

"One day i was on the bed of hospital, it was 13th day after Viraat's death, i hvnt talked to anyone for those 13 days, neither cried, nor expressed the feelings. Suddenly I heard a voice calling sonu, i can clearly hear it . . . . yes it was Viraat's voice . . . voice repeated again 'sonu' . . . i started looking here and there but no one was there . . . suddenly i felt something . . . . i don't know what it was but something entered within me . . . and i got a jerk . . . , my body shivered, but yes definitely something which wasn't visible to me had happened . . . i realised it was Viraat . . . he came to meet me . . . as per the rituals on 13th day the souls leave the earth and go back to heaven . . . . perhaps he came to say me adieu . . . That was the day when i cried . . . i cried . . . and i cried . . . ." and my heart said:

Life is a curse, without your company . . .
Smile is a curse, without your symphony . . .
Happiness is a curse, without your cheers . . .
Loneliness is a curse, without your tears . . .
Beauty is a curse, without your admiration . . .
Duty is a curse, without your obligations . . .
Womanhood is a curse, without your love . . .
Love is a curse, without your love . . .
Day is a curse, without your see . . .
Night is a curse, without your feel . . .
Feeling is a curse, without your presence . . .
Living is a curse, in your absence . . .
Eyes are a curse, without your glimpse . . .
Victory is a curse, without your triumphs . . .

"But then gradually I recollected my energy and I decided, if I can't die, if I can't win the battle of death, then i will win the battle of life. I decided that I will show life that if u r rude then am stronger than you to bear your adversities . . . I promised to myself that I will not be the sufferer. I promised to myself that I will no more pray that 'idol' which is called as God and my only dedication will be for my actions and deeds. I promised to myself that now I will laugh louder. I will live more life. I will take my own decisions and decided to pursue my higher studies. I decided to be a fighter instead of being a loser."

Kapil was frozen and stunned by hearing her. He was not able to believe his ears. His eyes got moistened.

"Kapil, are you listening?"

". . . ."

"Kapil, are you there?"

". . . ."

"hello, hello" and the call was disconnected by Kapil.

Nisaa tried to call him back but he didn't pick the call. Kapil had no words. He was so shocked to know about this bitter face of life. He sunk into his bed. He never expected this. One side he remembered Sharon's face and on the other side he thought about those hard things. He still wasn't able to connect the two. For a while he thought Nisaa just joked but no . . . it wasn't a joke. That It was a truth, a bitter truth. He was a guy who was born with a silver spoon. He never encountered such a situation. In just one day, he came to know about two deadliest news of his life and that too about the person whom he respects most and another whom he loves most. This was the first time he felt life is so hard, life is a cheater, first day he realised that his life was so simple. He just tried to recollect all the moments since when Sharon entered his life. He never felt that the cute face had hidden so much of pain behind it, her cool attitude never displayed her fear of losing loved ones, her confidence never displayed her despair, her shining bright eyes never displayed her sadness, her colourful attire never displayed her colorless life. It was difficult for him to decide was she a better actor or he was a bad observer. He always perceived her as the most cool, confident, intelligent, hot and sexy girl in the campus, but he never knew that this can be her past. Now he can understand her feelings better. He was now feeling more sorry for his act, but he still loved her. His feelings hasn't yet changed. He still wanted to have her, despite of her past. And he didn't know when he slept with such thoughts.

Saloni was quite and her eyes were moistened . . . . the only thing she can utter was, "is this a true story or a fiction?". But the professor didn't reply, he just asked her to wait till the story gets finished.

Professor could understand her state of mind. And then the flight has reached Delhi airport and it landed. Both Professor and Saloni came to the waiting room of the airport as the next flight from Delhi to Pune was after half an hour. Saloni was still silent and quiet, seeing which Professor brought some cold drinks and snacks for both of them. She had some snacks and then she was okay. And the moment she recovered herself, her first question was, "And sir what happe . . . ."

But the professor this time was busy with the Times Of India, today's newspaper. Saloni couldn't disturb him. She passed her half an hour of time anyhow by eating her snacks having cold drinks, taking snaps of few celebrities whom she discovered on the airport. And thus half an hour passed and the flight for Pune was ready.

Operator made an announcement and all the passengers including Professor and Saloni proceeded towards their flight and once again they were directed to their seats by a hot air hostess, this time Saloni has talked to her in advance for a seat near to Professor. And in no time, she was beside Professor, Now, professor was not surprised at all, because he knew she will not leave him, unless he dictates the whole story, It was sharp 12:30 p.m. and plane had took off.

Professor was looking through the window the plane was passing through the clouds. As the plane touches the clouds with its force, they drift apart and disappear, this reminds him of someone whose life was getting changed by the presence of someone and he again started . . . .

Portfolio Theory

The class was full packed and murmur was in the air, there was confusion floating across . . . suddenly Prof Shashank entered. Students could figure out that he had lost quite a good amount of weight. His face looked pale and wrinkled, he was not well. The news which was around about his health was confirmed.

Shashank greeted with effort "Good Morning Friends and how are you doing". There was a sheepish reply "Good Morning Sir", it was a concerned quit pro.

Professor started "Friends now we have very few lectures left most probably we shall be able to complete the whole module in couple of session. Today we shall start the Portfolio Management and its evaluation."

The Class was listening but nothing was getting into their head as all were thinking about his health and wanted to know how they can help him, they did not want to loose him at any cost. They also knew arranging such an enormous amount for his treatment was not a cake walk.

Sharon, Kapil and their friends had visited the Doctor the other day and they were told that he can be cured, but the expenses on the treatment is very costly as they have to take him to US for the complete treatment and process which will cost fortune. They needed at least 60 lacs and it was a really a huge amount for them.

Professor started the lecture. Though students were not in mood to study but they don't want to disappoint professor, for they knew teaching is not just bread butter for him but is a passion. He will be happy, if they will participate.

It started with the question, "Sir, I have a doubt, when Company does well, I mean gives good results still the share price falls. I really fail to understand why it happens. Is price of any scrip in market is just a fluke' enquired Chandu.

"It is a slightly complex issue, but before i touch upon the real facts and factors which determines the prices of stock, we need to understand certain market theories i.e. Market Efficiency Theory" said Shashank. Though he was not as energetic as he used to be but still his passion remains.

Kapil asked "Sir many times I have heard on TV specially on CNBC the anchor Udayan Mukherjee say the news is factored in, what does it mean". He started though his concentration was on Sharon, to see her face and her expressions, if she is okay.

Professor replied "Factored in means the prices are discounted or raised keeping the news in account. There is a concept called Market Efficient Theory".

Kapil asked "Can you tell me little more?".

Professor sat on the chair and replied "Efficient market hypothesis (EMH) is an idea partly developed in the 1960s by Eugene Fama. It states that it is impossible to beat the market because prices already incorporate and reflect all relevant information. This is also a highly controversial and often disputed theory. Supporters of this model believe it is pointless to search for undervalued stocks or try to predict trends in the market through fundamental analysis or Technical analysis. Under the efficient market hypothesis, any time you buy and sell securities, you're engaging in a game of chance, not skill. If markets are efficient and current, it means that prices always reflect all information, so there's no way you'll ever be able to buy a stock at a bargain price. This theory has been met with a lot of opposition, especially from the technical analysts. Their argument against the efficient market theory is that many investors base their expectations on past prices, past earnings, track records and other indicators. Because stock prices are largely based on investor expectation, many believe it only makes sense to believe that past prices influence future prices.

Formally, the level of efficiency of a market is characterized as belonging to one of the following (i) weak-form efficiency (ii) semi-strong form efficiency (iii) strong form efficiency."

Professor shared the slide.

Weak-form Market Efficiency

The weak-form efficiency comes into act when the consecutive price changes (returns) are uncorrelated in the market. This shows that the information available in public has no impact on the market and the prices.

Semi-strong Market Efficiency

The semi-strong form of efficiency shows that all information available in public are factored in and gets reflected in the prices. Hence, in such scenarios impact of positive information about the stock would lead to an instantaneous increase (decrease) in the prices. It also signifies that no investor would be able to outperform the market with trading strategies based on publicly available information.

Strong Market Efficiency

This efficiency is ideally desired by any market. Such efficiency would imply that both publicly available information and privately (non-public) available information are fully reflected in the prices instantaneously and no one can earn excess returns.

However there are evidence over the past two decades suggests that during many cases the markets are not efficient even in the weak form.

'**Professor,** What you have been talking so far i.e. investing in stock market seems risky, now how someone can reduce risk?' enquired Chabbi

'If you keep all eggs in a basket and if khali mistakenly sits on it, what you can expect' a big O Mess' Haa haa' Shashank was laughing. "That was PJ" said Vihaan. Students saw his laugh which shows how hard it was for him to smile. But they accompanied him.

'You can't afford to put all your money in one type of instrument like shares, bonds or any other instrument. You need to allot money to each instrument keeping lots of variable in considerations. They are

Risk taking capacity of the Investor
Age of the Investor

Govt Policies
Market Conditions etc' said Shashank

'Let me tell you some of the Portfolio Theories which may interest you and can be used practically to design your own portfolio.' Prof. Shashank started explaining. Suddenly all students become attentive the term 'your own portfolio' was something that they needed. Sharon immediately started jotting down his each and every word and others as well.

Professor started explaining. Students were listening to him quietly and carefully.

In early 1960s there was much contemplation among investment professionals about risk and its implications on selecting specific securities and other types of assets when constructing an optimum portfolio. Yet there were no effective means or models of measuring risk available at the time.

Prompted by the requirement, Harry Markowitz introduces premilinary portfolio model. The Portfolio selection model identifies an investor's undue risk, return preferences.

The Theory is base oncertain assumptions regarding investor behaviour

Investors consider each investment alternative as being represented by aprovbability distribution of expected returns over some holding period.

Individual estimate risk on the basis of the variability of expected returns.

Investors maximise one period expected utility and possess utility curve, which demonstrates diminishing marginal utility of wealth.

For agiven risk level, investor orefer high returns to lower returns. Similarly for a given level of expected return, investor prefer less risk to more risk. He suggested that diversification reduces the unsystematic risk component of the portfolio.

Kapil asked "How we can manage right way of investment and get maximum returns?."

Professor replied" It's through optimum Asset Allocation, the important task of appropriately allocating your available investment funds among different assets classes can seem daunting, with so many securities to choose from. Here we will illustrate what asset allocation is, its importance and how you can determine your appropriate asset mix and maintain it."

Shashank explained "What is Asset Allocation?

Asset allocation refers to the strategy of dividing your total investment portfolio among various asset classes, such as stocks, bonds and money market securities. Essentially, asset allocation is an organized and effective method of diversification. The diversification can be easily done using Portfolio Theory.

He further said "There are few issues with Modern Portfolio Theory. Modern portfolio theory shows that specific risk can be removed through diversification. The trouble is that diversification still doesn't solve the problem of systematic risk; even a portfolio of all the shares in the stock market can't eliminate that risk. Therefore, when calculating a deserved return, systematic risk is what plagues investors most.

He started explaining "The traditional beliefs is that diversification involves not putting all eggs in one basket". The policy involves as many baskets as possible; carried tothe extreme, it is good to have as many companies as possible and as many industries possible in one portfolio.

There are some expected methods of diversification

Randomness in selection of industries and companies: The probability of reducing risk is more with a random selection as the statistical error of choosing wrong companies will come down due to randomness of selection which is statistical technique. This involves placing of companies in order and picking them in random manner.

Optimisation of Selection Process: Given the amount of money to be invested there is optimum number of companies where money can be invested. If the number is too small, risk cannot bereduced adequetly and if the number is too big there will be diseconomies and difficulty of supervision, analysis and monitoring will increase risk again.

Markowitz diversification: He emphasised the need of right number of securities—not too many or too less and securities which are negatively correlated or not correlated at all. The purpose of diversification is to reduce the unsystematic risk arising our of company's policies and performance. Thus many of the risk can be reduced by proper choice of companies and industries.

One of the student asked "Sir what are the factors which influence Portfolio selection?". Professor replied"

Security: An investor is not prepared to loose money. So the security of the investment becomes an important issue. Here the security stands for maintenance of the capital value of the investment, atleast in nominal terms.

Return: The expected return is also very important considerations. Money put into investment is expected to earn a satisfactory rate of return. A satisfactory return compatibility with safety is thus the normal expectations of the customer.

Growth Prospects: The returns from the investment should not be only satidfactory but also should grow with time.

Liquidity: It refers to convertibility of investment back to cash at short notice.

Risk: Onvestors generally want amaximum gains with as minimum risk as possible.

Professor was amused as he completed the class there was no question raised during his session. Students looked as if their mind was somewhere else.

The lecture seemed to be lengthy to all, but they all had the information they require, especially Sharon and Kapil. Professor was explaining the lesson and then suddenly bell ranged and first times it so happened that students without wishing Professor ran out and went straight to the amphitheatre. Professor was shocked, he could sense that he miserably failed to maintain interest and that too in his penultimate class. He thought may be because of his poor health he could not generate the vigour and anxiety in the students. But that was the case he could not help.

There at Amphitheatre, there was not a single seat available, fully jam packed. All students of Professor Shashank were present, those who had heard of him were also there. Suddenly Sharon rose from her seat and with her Kapil and other Friends.

Sharon said "Friends you must be knowing why we are here, I don't want to go into intricacies, we need 50 lacs to bring Prof Shashank back. We need to take him to US for treatment and all this will require 50 lacs and I request all of you to donate generously. Give us whatever you have".

The students roared, there was chaos, everyone started asking what has happened to Professor, will the Lung Transplant be successful, what is the rate of success, will he be permanently cured. There were enormous questions, in between few of them shouted nobody can take Professor away from us not even death, we shall defeat death.

In one voice the Students shouted, we shall give everything and whatever we have to save Professor, money cannot become hurdle in his treatment.

Sharon said "Fine friends this is what we were expecting from all of you. Now we shall start collecting money from today onwards. I think we can finish in few days."

"Yes we will do it", roared students in one voice.

Portfolio Evaluation

One week had passed since collection of money commenced. Today was the last day for the money to be deposited. They had approached the management for some assistance. All the students were curious to know how much they have been able to collect, but at the same time they cannot afford to miss their favourite professor's last lecture. So the students moved to the classroom. The bell rang.

The doctor was right, Professor looked more weaker today. His body which always used to be straight looked a bit bent he took the help of a stick to walk. His face had completely drooped down. Students were crying at their heart to see their professor in this condition. They had high regards for such a great teacher, who came to fulfil his duty, even in this condition. Today it was the last lecture and then syllabus was finished.

He came and sat on the chair, and used collar mike for the deliberations and started. And here came the first question from Kapil "Sir is there any way by which we can evaluate and measure performance of the Portfolio which has been designed?".

Yes, there are ways by which it can be done" said Prof. Shashank.

He started explaining "Portfolio evaluation is the last step in the process of portfolio management. Portfolio amnalysis, selection and revision are undertaken with the objective of maximising returns and minimising risk. Portfolio evaluation is the stage where we examine to what extent the objective is achieved. Through Portfolio evaluation the investor finds out how well the securities have performed.

Portfolio Evaluation refers to the evaluation of the performance of the portfolio. It is essentially the process of comparing the return earned on a portfolio with the return earned on one or more other portfolios or on the benchmark portfolio. It comprises to functions Performance Measurement and Performance Evaluation.

Performance Measurement is an accounting function which measures the return earned on a portfolio during holding period or investment period.

Performance Evaluation on the other hand addresses such issues as whether the performance was superior or inferior and whether the performance was due to skill of the investor or just by chance, luck.

While evaluating the performance of aportfolio, the return earned on the portfolio has to be evaluated in the context of the risk associated with that portfolio. One approach would be to group portfolios into equivalent risk classes and then compare returns of the portfolios with each risk category. An alternative approach would be to pecifically adjust the return for the riskiness of the portfolio by developing risk adjusted return measures and use these for evaluating portfolios across different risk levels.

Shashank said," The Bottom Line of Portfolio performance measures should be a key aspect of the investment decision process. These tools provide the necessary information for investors to assess how effectively their money has been invested (or may be invested). Remember, portfolio returns are only part of the story. Without evaluating risk-adjusted returns, an investor cannot possibly see the whole investment picture, which may inadvertently lead to clouded and fishy investment decisions.

And here ends the last lecture of the session. Professor wished all the students for their bright future and gave them blessings, some students came to touch his feet for his blessings, some hugged him, some even kissed him. Professor and all the students became emotional. Professor was emotional perhaps he knew this is his last meeting with his students and students were emotional because they knew what hard times professor is going through, though no one can share their feelings. Then the professor left and all the students as well.

Few minutes later Sharon, Kapil, Chabbi and few of the students involved in collection met again at Amphithetre.

Sharone said "Friends i had guessed right, we could generate approximately 10 lacs, we have approached the college management also, they are overwhelmed by the support extended by the students for the noble cause and so would like to release 10 lacs from Founder Presidents Fund. but maximum we can go is 20 lacs and there is a huge gap, a gap of 30 Lacs."

Today was supposed to be full jam packed sessions from visiting faculties but students have announced that they won't be attending as they had some important work to do. Management knew, what was going on and so the sessions were cancelled.

Amphitheatre was packed again there was not a single chair which was empty, this has never happened in the history of the college.

Kapil started saying "Friends thanks for your generous help but before he could speak further one student shouted . . . "Stop the crap can you tell us how much you were able to collect?". Everyone was anxious to know whether the job was done.

Kapil started saying, students knew that something was wrong, he was not confident.

"Friends with great effort and generous donation from management, we could garner only 20 lacs and we still require 30 more to make it good. Further we also don't have much time as the treatment and transplant procedure need to start in a duration of four months. So it's not only money but we are also fighting with time". There was a cold silence as if everyone were wiped down by cold avalanche wave. For few seconds, nobody opened their mouth to speak then one student spoke softly "Now what next, there has to be some solution to this issue".

Sharon rose from her seat "Yes friends there is a huge problem and that is why we are here to resolve the same. We would like to take opinion of everyone on how to go about further".

"Why not take loan from bank, we can put our assets as mortgage and against that Bank can pay us required amount" said one of the students.

Kapil replied "Friends unfortunately Manager knows what we are up to and he has simply refused to accept anything like bank loan through mortgage etc."

Nobody had any answer because collecting another 30 lacs was next to impossible as they had exhausted every possible avenue they had. One student shouted why not give this amount to stock broker and ask him to make 20 lacs to 50 lacs.

Sharon said "We have already tried this option but there are no brokers who are confident of doing that."

"Forget the brokers, we will do it. Professor always used to say there are unlimited returns in stock market. Let us do it and with God's grace and pure intentions behind the work, i am sure we will succeed."

The statement looked like a war cry from Hindi war movie or melodrama dialogue from Ramlila or Mahabaharat. All were quiet and there was a pin drop silence for few minutes.

Kapil voice raised "You are right buddy, let's us do it ourselves, i don't think so we have any other option, we have to do it and we will do it".

And then there were hundreds of students shouting in a one voice let us do it. One of the students shouted "Kapil why not you and Sharon take the lead?. We all will help you and whatever way you want us to."

All of the students shouted yes" Kaps and Sharone will do it. We all will support them. But yes they have to do it".

Kapil calmed down the students and glanced at Sharon, Chabbi and his friends. There was a silent acknowledgement in their eyes. He said "Ok friends we shall take the responsibility and try something which looks impossible as of now, however stock market is the place were impossible becomes possible".

Sharon said "Friends we will try our best and keep you updated. Let us hope we succeed in our mission and by God's grace we will come out triumphant".

Kapil was smiling because this was the first time that Sharon has sweared by God or has anyway acknowledged it.

Sharon said "Friends we need to start working on the project immediately. It's going to be a daunting task. We shall need help from many of you. We need to work in teams and within next seven days we have to ensure that money is invested in the market then only we have any chance to make it to what we intend to."

She was speaking like a General at war front, as if her husband's spirit has entered her body. Within couple of hours the team were set and settled.

There were two teams. One was lead by Ashok and Chabbi who would go and check out with those brokers who would charge them minimum brokerage and would give facility like x times investment on their corpus.

The other team was of Kapil and Sharon, who would design the formula for investment and execute it.

The meeting was disbursed, Students shouted with full throttle of their voice "Ganapati Bappa Morya, Jai Mata Di, we shall do it and we will".

The teams had very limited time to get into action. The team lead by Ashok had comparatively easy job but Sharone and Kapil had to climb a mountain and they knew if they succeed they will get hero's reception if they fail they will be buried without trace.

The job was on and they had to work together to ensure they give their best effort. Kapil had always suggested Sharon that they make deadly combination. He often said 1 + 1 in their case is 11 and not 2. The time had come to prove that.

Sharon said to Kapil "What are you thinking?". Kapil said "Same thing what is there in your mind, we have to save our Professor and for that even if we have to invent all together new genre of trading funda, we have to do it." Everyone dispersed for their respective tasks.

A Way to Discovery!!

Next day morning at 10, Kapil and Sharon met at the Library. They took out every book on stock market and all were scattered on table.

Kapil asked Sharon "What should be the game plan, how we have to go ahead?".

Sharon replied "See Professor has always emphasised on long term investment he never wanted us to go for Intraday or to the matter of fact try derivatives. However we are in such a situation that time is our enemy had it been question of few more months or years to arrange money, we would have gone with the Long term or mid term investment Plan. But now we don't have any other option than to have plan which will be mix of Intraday, option and long term investment.".

"You are right" said Kapil. "Also we need to decide on how much to be allocated for intraday, options and buying assets."

They both again immersed into books, journals and newspapers. Kapil and Sharon had opened their Laptops, the coffee was served by the canteen man. Librarian had gone giving them the keys. They both were discussing and writing on paper and then checking something on computer and used to throw paper in dustbin. The canteen person served their lunch and the dinner both in the library itself. They had it and again engaged themselves into the book, Kapil almost had got a new hairstyle by notching them again and again each time he get became confused, Sharon had got all her pencils stuck into her bun. Canteen person has also closed the canteen, he gave them few water bottles to drink, that was in fact used by Kapil and Sharon to keep their eyes open, to avoid sleep. All the books were laid on the floor, table, chair as if it is not a library but a storeroom. They kept on working like mad, as if they had decided that they will not leave the library unless they find. The clock strikes 2 A.M. in the night.

Suddenly Kapil shouted "Yes yes yes its working, it can work, it will work, it has to work". He jumped out of the chair on to the Library table pulled Sharon up and lifted her, he was swinging her with joy, though Sharon was a bit perturbed by Kapil's sudden reaction but she was also very happy for the same reason, her bun loosened and her hair started rolling on her face, all the pencils fall on the floor. After a second, realizing the situation Kapil released Sharon off his arms, Sharon felt a bit shy but without losing any seconds they get back to their task. They had come out with something which both believed will work. "We did it Sharon, we did it." Kapil said in an excited voice, "Yes, we did!!" Sharon replied with the same energy level, recollecting herself from what happened seconds ago. They were back testing their formula and finally it was giving them the desired result. But they also knew that whenever there is extraordinary situation or out of blue moon something strange happens, the formula or the strategy may fail. They kept their fingers crossed.

The Decision was that 50% of the amount will be invested in options as they were not so sure of intraday, further option gives them sufficient time to alter strategy incase of extraordinary situation.

The 25% would be invested into stocks for a month and remaining 25 % would be again into options but the strategy would be a safer one with approximate target of 15% return.

They also needed help from the Third team who could design software for them to use. The software had to capture data from NSE website and utilise it for themselves. The lag time had to be minimum as the trend can change sharply and they have to act fast to get the desired result.

Sharon takes out her cellphone and rings a number "Ramesh, get up it's morning". Ramesh watches his cellphone and shouts "You idiot it is 3 am night".

Sharon talks calmly "We got the formula, it is giving us result, its morning for us and now pull up your jeans, zap you room and come to college Library immediately". There was authority in her voice and she meant what she had said to Ramesh. In fifteen minutes Ramesh was in Library.

He said "What the hell you are doing so late?".

"Not we but you are also here now and let's get the ball rolling" Kapil said in a super motivated tone.

Kapil explained Ramesh everything about their requirement. His much concern was that the software should pick data fast so that they can get the triggers without much time lag.

The formula for Options

The software will take a clue from Asean market and decide for the trend. In case the asean market has opened up then there are chances that NSE also opens positively unless there is extraordinary situation prevailing in India.

In case the trend is up the software indicates to buy Call option. They had decided to trade into Nifty option.

They would purchase Nifty Option at par . . . .

After every five minutes the software will draw Candle stick and will check EMA of 1 minute and 5 minutes and their crossover. If the 1 minute crossover crosses from down to up for 5 mts EMA and the Candle Stick is bullish in nature. There is buy signal and we shall go for buying Call option. If it is otherwise we shall sell Call Option and buy Put Option.

We will continue with the strategy for both Call and Put.

Formula for Mid term and Long Term Investment

Moving Averages 5 days EMA, and13 days EMA and/ or 5 days EMA and 26 days EMA positive crossover. We need to buy.

Moving Averages 5 days EMA and 13 days EMA and/ or 5 Days EMA and 26 days EMA negative crossover. We need to sell.

Check if any Bullish Price Pattern like Inverted head and Shoulder, Double Bottom, Rounding Bottom, Up Flag then we buy.

If Price Pattern is Bearish with Head and Shoulder, Double Top, Rounding Top and Down Flag then we sell.

Stochastic: the Crossover should be within 3 preceeding days.

If uptrend and positive crossover on the stochastic, we buy.

If downtrend and Negative crossover on stochastic then we sell.

MACD: The Crossover should be within 5 preceding days.

Positive Crossover in positive zone. We buy

Negative Crossover in negative zone. We sell.

Since for Long Term we can use websites like www. chartsin.com as time lag and quick decision minute wise is not required.

The Formula was clear and it was to be implemented.

Ramesh was on his work and he also had very limited time as he had to test whether it gives desired results as expected. Next day Ramesh meets his other team mates and they start working on the project. They were given 3 days to complete as 2 days would be required to check the efficiency of the software.

Finally Ramesh on the third day morning meets Kapil and Sharon and presents them the software.

Ramesh says "Buddy this is IndyStock pro it will do following things . . . .

Stock Watchlist—Current Stock Info
Stock Watchlist—Intraday Stock Price
Portfolio Management—Transaction Records
Portfolio Management—Cash Management
Portfolio Management—Dividend Management
Portfolio Management—Multiple Portfolios
Alert—SMS
Alert—System Tray
Indicator Filter—Indicator Installer
Indicator Filter—Indicator Editor
Indicator Filter—Indicator Scanner
Charting—History Stock Info
Charting—History Index Info
Charting—Portfolio Summary
Charting—Cash Flow Summary
Customising Charts and Calculating results and counts

Ramesh had incorporated everything taught by Professor which helps in selecting right stock to invest. The software had used funadamental Analysis and

Technical Charts at realtime to get the best possible investement opportunities.

Ramesh said" The software will get connected to BSE/NSE website and will collect data at realtime. It will also generate Technical Charts backend and trigger points using fundamental Analysis. We just have to fix criterion for our selection of stock and it will give us five best options."

"Wow thats great You have done Buddy" Sharon was excited and so was Kapil. Finally they had the Bramhastra in their hand which would fulfil their dream. They kept on testing on Nifty options and various other Stock options and the results were great. Two days they had invested notionally and checked the results. They were satisfied and were ready for final assault.

Saturday again all met at their regular meeting spot Amphitheatre.

Ashok and his team was ready with the details of the brokers, though they could manage for few only, then Sharon revealed that she also does a part time work as a broker, she can also assist them in that matter. They all were happy, surprised and astonished had mixed expressions, but they had less time to express it, So, they all moved for the next step of investments as per their planning.

They applied there whole fundas and philosophies they have formulated . . . . with a bit of doubt and risk, because they don't have other options.

After Four months . . . .

The flight for United States of America was scheduled at 1:45p.m. in the afternoon. All the students were busy in making arrangements for the professor's visit to the world's best surgeon, Professor was accompanied by a team of experts from India. His closest Raghu also accompanied him, in his toughest mission.

Yes, those so called kids/students have made it!!! They managed to make 60 lakhs out of those 20 lakhs. First time after those mishaps Sharon thanked God, all the students were glad that they had managed to collect that much amount of money. All the students came to the professor to give him the bestest of wishes they can. They all wished him. It was the last stage of the Professor, this transplantation was the only hope left, Professor's health had deteriorated a lot, he had lost his memory power miserably, he wasn't even able to recognise few of his students whom he used to call with names in the classroom, his skin has stuck to his bones, his eyes, skin and his body has paled to yellowish colouration, his belly has protruded more, he has become too thin, a musty odour, which is perhaps due to some particular chemical, has become his part, don't know how few of his fingers had deformed, again a side effect of this deadly disease. Students were very scared to see their professor in this condition. Professor was being fed through food pipe which was inserted through his nose. A saline was permanently given to him. Everyone just wished for the well being of their professor. A cab was booked for the whole team and a bus was booked for the students. All the students came to the airport to see him off.

Doctors thanked the students and assured them they will be successful. They left the students in tears and moved ahead for the biggest surgery a miracle in waiting . . . . The students did not know whether this was their last meeting with the professor or will they be able to meet him again . . . . the thought of losing their professor broke them, but there was no other option left with them, they have to wait and wait . . . . that's it . . . .

The plane landed and had reached the Pune airport. Saloni was still in the confusion that narration done by the Mr. Ranade was a story or a real life incident. There was still a suspense for her that whether the doctors were able to save that Professor or not and what happened about the love stories of Vihaan and Chhabi and was Kapil able to convince Sharon. Everything was still a suspense for her. She was still in her own thoughts when she realised that they have collected their luggages and reached the main gate of the airport. She thought is this the end of my journey, will the professor tell me about the rest part or not. Suddenly her thoughts were interrupted by a group of young boys and girls, as they proceeded towards the Mr. Ranade and raised him and put him on their shoulders and started shouting, "Hip hip hurray! Hip hip hurray!" They put so many garlands on him and greeted him with loud pomp and show. Saloni thought they might be the fans, and then after many request of Mr. Ranade, they get him down. And again hugged him as if they were very close to him. Saloni was just about to ask Mr. Ranade about them, then professor introduced her to all, "Meet, Miss Saloni, she is a journalist. She came with me all along from Singapore just to take my interview. Must say u r a very sincere girl, Miss Saloni." Saloni gave a meek smile.

Then Professor introduced all the young people standing there to Saloni. He started with the person on the extreme right, he was smart and charming, "He is

Vihaan, your character of the book." Professor gave a smile and winked at her.

Saloni was standing with eyes wide open. Professor started, "And she is . . . ."

"Chhabi, right. She is as cute as you told me." Professor smiled as Saloni said.

And then one by one she recognized all Ashok, Nisaa, and others and then she came to the last boy standing on the extreme left, with light beard, his masculine and fit body resembled him with Kapil and Saloni was right in all her guesses. Suddenly she said, "and where is the Professor? I expected him also here." With her words everyone present there started laughing . . . . Mr. Ranade was also smiling, suddenly Saloni realised something, "OMG . . . . sooo . . . ." "Yes, miss I am Professor Shashank as per you book" replied Mr. Ranade and started laughing . . . Saloni was amused to hear all this, she felt as if she had cracked a puzzle. She was so happy to see this.

Suddenly Vihaan said, "Sir, on your grand welcome I would like to make an announcement." Professor gave a smile and pointed his hand to proceed, "Sir, with yours and our parents' permission, we have decided to become one." Holding Chhabi in his arms, she felt a bit shy. And as he completed his sentence there was a loud hooting, whistling and everyone congratulated Vihaan and Chhabi . . . . and Saloni was so happy to hear this, she hugged Chhabi and gave her many congratulations, but her eyes were still searching for someone . . . . Sharon. Her mind was occupied with the thoughts Where is she, How is she. If Kapil is here that means they aren't together. Busy with her thoughts, she looked towards the main gate of the airport. Suddenly she saw a flamboyant girl coming through the gate, she was in a very hurry, as if she was worried, if she can miss someone. Soon Saloni took her eyes off her and again she drowned in her thoughts. In a seconds, she realize is she SHARON . . . . and she again looked towards the girl, yes that was a girl with brown hair the strands flowing on her face, her tight jeans, loose pink net shirt with spaghetti beneath with a shoulder bag. Saloni's happiness increased with every step that girl moved towards her, she came nearer, Saloni 's heart was beating faster and as soon as she arrived near the professor, Saloni almost shouted, "Look, Sharon is here." Everyone stared towards Sharon. Everyone was astonished to see her. Since last day of college, she never contacted anyone. No one can find her location, nor even Kapil, nor Nisaa, but only Professor knew where she was. Sharon went straight to the professor and wished him for his achievement, everyone asked her where she had been. Sharon just smiled and said she is doing well. Amongst all, Kapil was the only one who was standing in one corner and still looking at her or can say admire her, he stood like a statue, he dreamt of her every night but cannot see her, he has been dying since last two years to see her, suffering to listen her voice, he has passed his everyday beginning with the hope that he will be able to find her, everyday he slept by consoling his heart that if you love her, you will get her, each day his heart cried and punished himself by hurting himself for his loss . . . he had passed his two years like a dreadful night. Today when she was in front of him, his eyes were confused, whether to see her or to fill it with tears. He wanted to just hold her and to tell her that how much he loved her. Sharon, though busy in talking to others, her eyes also watched him with corner of eye. She can see the pain and sadness in Kapil's eyes. Both the eyes communicated the same thing, but she was not in the situation to say something. It had been two long years after the mishap, but still she wasn't able to move on in her life. She was bounded by her own philosophies, she felt herself in such a miserable situation, that she was wordless. This was the reason why two years back she decided to leave everything, she had dropped her MBA lectures and continued it with job. Yes, she had also fallen in love with Kapil, but she didn't have the courage to move on, she ran away from the situation, she tried to keep herself busy in something else, so that she shouldn't miss him. She stil felt that those mishaps are because of her and she cannot put someone's life in risk. She pretended to be strong but the fear of losing someone out shadowed her courage and she made such decision. She just wanted to let Kapil understand her. As they were busy in their thoughts, soon Saloni came to Sharon and asked, "How are you? I have never met a brave girl like you. Nice meeting you." Sharon gave a meek smile in response. "So, howzz ur life goin on?" Saloni added.

"Yups, perfect"

"Sure, I mean . . . . a . . . . anything new"

"A . . . . a . . . . nothing new, as it is, yeah recently i have been promoted for the post of Technical analyst in one of the broking firm."

"Ohh . . . Gud . . . thats really great congratulations . . ."

Meanwhile the professor went to Kapil and said something in his ear. Sharon could see that, but she ignored it. Soon she found Kapil coming towards her. In a seconds she found herself so uncomfortable, her heart started beating faster, she wished to run away, she even tried but Saloni held her hand and soon Kapil was just a step far from her. Saloni has now let go off Sharon's hand and wanted to be the witness of a great day. Kapil was looking at Sharon. Sharon first tried to avoid him, she was struggling with her fist, but soon she can't avoid her eyes to look at his. Both looked into each other's eyes, there was a silent communication in their eyes and they both can feel the silence.

Kapil wanted to hug her and Sharon wanted Kapil to hug her . . . in seconds "Sharon" Kapil said, there was a loud pain that was dying to tell her about his sufferings. That simple word brought tears in the eyes of both and then Kapil just hugged her and Sharon was in his arms. Both cried . . . . their eyes were today free to flow without any dams . . . . their souls which suffered till now also felt the smoothness of love, they kissed each other on their foreheads and cheeks and just kept themselves in their arms, as if now they won't allow each other to leave them. But soon they realized and regained senses, they drifted apart. Sharon felt shy, it was first time when Kapil saw her shy face. He was extremely glad to see her. He immediately knelt down and while offering his hand towards Sharon said, "Will you be part of my life, part of me, with me, for me, in me . . . . always . . . . forever . . . . never to leave me . . . . I will be your lover throughout my life, Am multitasking and can change my roles as per requirement . . . . i will be the care taker, i will be the husband, i will be the father, i will be yours forever . . . . So, now please hire me as your full time lover . . . . U r my dream destination . . . . Am giving exams for this job since last two years and i want to pass it anyhow . . . . I love you . . . . Would u like to be my love . . . ." There was a loud clap in the arena, as he ended. All the passengers, gate keepers, public have gathered there and all were waiting for Sharon's reply and she said and acted like a beautiful damsel, "Ok, u r hired from right now and ur first task is to kiss me . . . . on my lips . . ." Sharon pointed on her lips like a seducing actress. And there was a big applause, hooting and whistles all around. Kapil in a second pulled her up and gave her a big smooch. Professor, Saloni and all the students were witness of this great incident and everyone blessed the couple for their bright and safe future. Saloni was clapping with the tears in her eyes . . . . Now she knew that the story wasn't a fiction but a legend . . . and it was the same professor who had been snatched from the death by his students, his dear students, who loved him more than just a professor.